SACRED READING

for Lent 2017

SACRED READING

for Lent 2017

Apostleship of Prayer

Douglas Leonard, Executive Director

Ave Maria Press   AVE   Notre Dame, Indiana

© 2016 by the Apostleship of Prayer

All rights reserved. No part of this book may be used or reproduced in any manner whatsoever, except in the case of reprints in the context of reviews, without written permission from Ave Maria Press®, Inc., P.O. Box 428, Notre Dame, IN 46556, 1-800-282-1865.

Founded in 1865, Ave Maria Press is a ministry of the United States Province of Holy Cross.

www.avemariapress.com

Paperback: ISBN-13 978-1-59471-699-7

E-book: ISBN-13 978-1-59471-700-0

Cover image © Thinkstock.

Cover and text design by David Scholtes.

Printed and bound in the United States of America.

CONTENTS

INTRODUCTION

In the gospel, Jesus says his disciples will fast when he, the Bridegroom, is taken from them. We know that Jesus is always with us, but during the season of Lent we honor him in a special way by entering a forty-day period of prayer, fasting, and almsgiving in preparation for the celebration of the resurrection of the Lord, Easter Sunday. The season of Lent begins on Ash Wednesday, dividing the cycle of Ordinary Time in the Church year. Sundays in Lent are not counted as fast days. Fast days continue through Holy Saturday, the day before Easter. Lent officially ends on Holy Thursday, the beginning of the Easter triduum.

The number of days of Lent corresponds to the forty days Jesus prayed and fasted in the desert before beginning his earthly ministry. Lent is a time to allow God to help us become holy, to help us look to the needs of others and minister to those needs, and most of all, to grow in faith, hope, and love, for those virtues are of God, motivating and empowering us to live the Gospel.

One of the important ways Christians observe Lent is by taking up—or practicing with greater intentionality—certain devotional or prayer practices to help them prepare to celebrate the Easter feast with greater joy. Christians throughout the world are rediscovering a powerful, ancient form of prayer known as sacred reading (lectio divina) that invites communion with God through scripture reading and contemplation. What better way to deepen one's friendship with Jesus Christ, the Word of God, than by prayerfully encountering him in the daily gospel reading?

Sacred reading is a spiritual practice that, guided by the Holy Spirit, invites you to interact with the words of the daily gospel. As you read and pray this way, you may find—as many others have—that the Lord speaks to you in intimate and surprising ways. The reason for this is simple: as we open our hearts to Jesus, he opens his heart to us.

St. Paul prays beautifully for his readers:

> For this reason I bow my knees before the Father, from whom every family in heaven and on earth takes its name. I pray that, according to the riches of his glory, he may grant that you may be strengthened in your inner being with power through his Spirit, and that Christ may dwell in your hearts through faith, as you are being rooted and grounded in love. I pray that you may have the power to comprehend, with all the saints, what is the breadth and length and height and depth, and to know the love of Christ that surpasses knowledge, so that you may be filled with all the fullness of God. (Eph 3:14–19)

This book moves you through each day's gospel by prompting you at each step of lectio divina, getting you started with reading, observing, praying, listening, and resolving to act. But most important is your own response to the Word and the Spirit for that is how you will grow in your relationship with Jesus. If you are sincerely seeking God, the Holy Spirit will lead you in this process.

How to Use This Book

This book will set you on a personal prayer journey with Jesus from Ash Wednesday through the end of Holy Week. Please note that some of the readings in this booklet have been shortened for group use. The citation for shortened readings will first show the reading that is included in the book and will then show the citation for the day's complete reading in parentheses.

In prayerful reading of the daily gospels, you join your prayers with those of believers all over the world. Following the readings for Lent, you will be invited to reflect on the gospel text for the day in six simple but profound steps:

1. Know that God is present with you and ready to converse.

At all times God is everywhere, including where you are in this very moment. The human mind is incapable of fully grasping the mystery of God, but we do know some things about God from scripture. God is the transcendent ground of all being, invisible, eternal, and infinite in power. God is Love, with infinite love for you and me. God is one with and revealed through the Word, Jesus Christ, who became flesh. Through him all things were made, and by him and for him all things subsist. Jesus is the Way, the Truth, and the Life. He says that those who know him also know his Father. Through the passion, death, and resurrection of Jesus, we are reconciled with God. If we believe in Jesus Christ, we become the sons and daughters of Almighty God.

God gives us the Holy Spirit to lead us to truth and understanding. The Holy Spirit also gives us power to live obedient to the teachings of Jesus. The Holy Spirit draws us to prayer and works in us as we pray. No wonder we come into God's presence with gladness. All God's ways are good and beautiful. We can get to know God better by encountering God in the Word, which is Jesus himself.

The prompt prayer at the beginning of each day's reading is just that: a prompt, something to get you started. In fact, all the elements in the process of sacred reading are meant to prompt you to your own conversations with God. After reading the prompt, feel free to continue to pray in your own words: respond in your own way, pray in your own way, and hear God speaking to you personally. Your goal is to make sacred reading your own prayer time each day.

2. Read the gospel.

The entire Bible is the Word of God, but the gospels (Matthew, Mark, Luke, and John) specifically tell the good news about Jesus Christ. Throughout the Church year, the daily gospel readings during Mass will come from all four gospels. The Sacred Reading series (the prayer books as well as the seasonal booklets for Advent/Christmas and Lent/Easter) concentrates on praying with the daily gospels. These readings contain the story of Jesus' life, his teachings, his works, his passion and death on the Cross, his resurrection on the third day, and his ascension into heaven.

The gospels interpret Jesus' ministry for us. Much more, by the Holy Spirit, we can find in the gospels the very person of Jesus Christ. Prayerful reading of the daily gospel is an opportunity to draw close to the Lord: Father, Son, and Holy Spirit. As we pray with the gospels, we can be transformed by the grace of God—enlightened, strengthened, and moved. Seek to read the gospel with a complete openness to what God is saying to you. Many who pray with the gospel recommend rereading it several times.

3. Notice what you think and feel as you read the gospel.

Sacred reading can involve every faculty—mind, heart, emotions, soul, spirit, sensations, imagination, and much more—though usually not all at once. Different passages touch different keys in us. Sometimes we may laugh. Sometimes we may need to stop and worship before we continue. Sometimes we will be puzzled, amazed, stung, abashed, reminded of something lovely, or reminded of something we had wanted to forget.

Seek to feel all of your emotions as you read. Apply your intellect, too. You will confront problems of context and exegesis on a daily basis. That's okay. Sometimes you may experience very little. That's okay, too. God is at work anyway. Give yourself to the gospel and take from it what is there for you each day.

Most important, notice what in particular jumps out at you, whatever it may be. It may be a word, a phrase, a character, an image, a pattern, an emotion, a sensation—some arrow to your heart. Whatever it is, pay attention to it, because the Holy Spirit is using it to accomplish something in you.

Sometimes a particular gospel repeats during the liturgical year of the Church. To pray through the same gospel even on successive days presents no problem whatsoever to your sacred reading. St. Ignatius of Loyola, founder of the Jesuits and author of *The Spiritual Exercises*, actually recommends repeated meditation on passages of scripture. Read in the Spirit, gospel passages have unlimited potential to reveal to us the truths we are ready to receive. For the receptive soul, the Word of God has boundless power to illuminate and transform the prayerful believer.

4. *Pray as you are led for yourself and others.*

Praying is just talking with God. Believe God hears you. Believe God will answer you. Believe God knows what you need even before you ask. Jesus says so in the gospels. So your conversation with God can go far beyond asking for things. You may thank, praise, worship, rejoice, mourn, explain, question, reveal your fears, seek understanding, or ask forgiveness. Your conversation with God has no limits. God is the ideal conversationalist. God wants to spend much time with you.

Being human, we can't help being self-absorbed, but praying is not just about our own needs. We are often moved by the gospel to pray for others. We will regularly remember our loved ones in prayer. Sometimes we will be led to pray for someone who has hurt us. At other times we will be moved to pray for a class of people in need wherever they are in the world, like persecuted Christians, refugees, the mentally ill, the rich, teachers, the unborn, or the lonely.

We may also pray with the universal Church by praying for the pope's prayer intentions. Those intentions are entrusted to the Apostleship of Prayer and are available through its web site and its annual and monthly leaflets. You may get your own copy of this year's papal prayer intentions by contacting the Apostleship of Prayer. The Apostleship is the pope's worldwide prayer network, with more than thirty-five million members worldwide. Jesus asked us to unite in prayer, promising that the Father would grant us whatever we ask in his name.

5. Listen to Jesus.

Jesus the Good Shepherd speaks to his own sheep, who hear his voice (see Jn 10:27). This listening is a most wonderful time in your sacred reading prayer experience. The italicized words in this passage are the words I felt impressed upon my heart as I prayed with these readings. I included them in order to help you to listen more actively for whatever it is the Lord might be saying to you.

Jesus speaks to all in the gospels, but in your sacred reading prayer experience he can now speak exclusively to you. If you can, write down what he says to you and reread his words during the day. Put all of Jesus' words to you in a folder or keep a spiritual notebook. Believers through the ages have recorded the words of Jesus to them, holy mystics and ordinary believers alike.

It takes faith to hear the voice of Jesus. This faith will grow as you practice listening. Ideally, we will learn to hear what Jesus is saying to us all day long, as we face difficult situations perhaps. Listening to the voice of Jesus is practicing the presence of God. As St. Paul said, "In him we live and move and have our being" (Acts 17:28).

St. Ignatius of Loyola called this conversation with Jesus *colloquy*. That word simply means that two or more people are talking. St. Ignatius even urges us to include the saints in our prayer conversations. We believe in the Communion of Saints. If you have a patron saint, don't be afraid to talk to him or her. In her autobiography, St. Thérèse of Lisieux, who was a member of the Apostleship of Prayer, describes how she spoke often with Mary and Joseph as well as Jesus.

6. *Ask God to show you how to live today.*

Pope Benedict XVI commented that sacred reading is not complete without a call to action: something in our praying leads us to do something in our day. Perhaps we find an opportunity to serve, to love, to give, to lead, or to do something good for someone else. Perhaps we find occasion to repent, to forgive, to ask forgiveness, to make amends. Open your heart to anything God might want you to do. Try to keep the conversation with God going all day long.

Asking God to show you how to live is the last step of the sacred reading prayer time, but that doesn't mean you need to end it here. Keep it going. You may drift off in the presence of God, lose attention, or even fall asleep, but you can come back. God is always present with you, seeking to love you and to be loved. God is always seeking to lead us to green pastures. God is our strength, our rock, our ever-present help in time of trouble. God is full of mercy, ready to forgive us again and again. God sees us through very difficult times. God heals us. God gives his life to us constantly. God is our Maker, Father, Mother, Lover, Servant, Savior, and Friend. We know that from the gospel. He is an inexhaustible spring of blessing and holiness in our innermost selves. The sanctification of our souls is God's work, not our own.

As you read, ask the Holy Spirit to lead you in this process. With genuine faith, open yourself to respond to the Word and the Spirit, and your relationship with Jesus will continue to deepen and to grow just as the

infant Jesus grew within the womb of the Blessed
Mother. This in turn will lead you to share the love of
Christ with all those you encounter just as the Blessed
Mother draws all those who encounter her directly to
her Son.

Other Resources to Help You

These Sacred Reading resources, both the seasonal
booklets and the annual prayer book, are enriched by
the spirituality of the Apostleship of Prayer. Since 1844
our mission has been to encourage Catholics to pray
each day for the good of the world, the Church, and the
prayer intentions of the Holy Father. In particular, we
encourage Christians to respond to the loving gift of
Jesus Christ by making a daily offering of themselves
each day. As we give the Lord our hearts, we ask him
to make them like his own Heart, full of love, mercy,
and peace.

   These booklets may be used in small groups or
as a handy individual resource for those who want a
special way to draw close to Christ during Lent. If you
enjoy these reflections and would like to continue this
prayerful reading throughout the year, pick up a copy
of the *Sacred Reading* annual prayer guide. You can
order one through the Apostleship of Prayer website
or through avemariapress.com.

   These annual books offer a personal prayer experience that can be adapted to meet your particular needs.
For example, some choose to continue to reflect upon
each day's reading in writing, either in the book or in a
separate journal or notebook, to create a record of their

spiritual journey for the entire year. Others supplement their daily reading from the book with the daily videos and other online resources available through the Apostleship of Prayer website.

For more information about the Apostleship of Prayer and about the other resources we have developed to help men and women cultivate habits of daily prayer, visit our website at apostleshipofprayer.org.

I pray that this experience may help you walk closely with God every day.

Douglas Leonard, PhD
Executive Director
Apostleship of Prayer

We Need Your Feedback!
Ave Maria Press and the Apostleship of Prayer would like to hear from you. After you've finished reading, please go to **avemariapress.com/feedback** to take a brief survey about your experience with *Sacred Reading for Lent 2017*. We'll use your input to make next year's book even better.

WEEK OF ASH WEDNESDAY

Dear brothers and sisters, may this Lenten season find the whole Church ready to bear witness to all those who live in material, moral, and spiritual destitution the Gospel message of the merciful love of God our Father, who is ready to embrace everyone in Christ. We can do this to the extent that we imitate Christ who became poor and enriched us by his poverty. Lent is a fitting time for self-denial; we would do well to ask ourselves what we can give up in order to help and enrich others by our own poverty. Let us not forget that real poverty hurts: no self-denial is real without this dimension of penance. I distrust a charity that costs nothing and does not hurt.

Pope Francis
Lenten Message 2014

Wednesday, March 1, 2017
Ash Wednesday

Know that God is present with you and ready to converse.

"Lent has begun, Lord. Draw me nearer to yourself in this season. Open me fully to your Word."

Read the gospel: Matthew 6:1–6, 16–18.

Jesus said, "Beware of practicing your piety before others in order to be seen by them; for then you have no reward from your Father in heaven.

"So whenever you give alms, do not sound a trumpet before you, as the hypocrites do in the synagogues and in the streets, so that they may be praised by others. Truly I tell you, they have received their reward. But when you give alms, do not let your left hand know what your right hand is doing, so that your alms may be done in secret; and your Father who sees in secret will reward you.

"And whenever you pray, do not be like the hypocrites; for they love to stand and pray in the synagogues and at the street corners, so that they may be seen by others. Truly I tell you, they have received their reward. But whenever you pray, go into your room and shut the door and pray to your Father who is in secret; and your Father who sees in secret will reward you. . . .

"And whenever you fast, do not look dismal, like the hypocrites, for they disfigure their faces so as to show others that they are fasting. Truly I tell you, they have received their reward. But when you fast, put oil on your head and wash your face, so that your fasting may be seen not by others but by your Father who is in secret; and your Father who sees in secret will reward you."

Notice what you think and feel as you read the gospel.

Jesus says to pray, fast, and do good works in secret, for to do them before others undercuts their spiritual value. When we desire that others think well of us, we tend to become hypocrites. We should trust God for our reward.

Pray as you are led for yourself and others.

"Lord, help me keep secrets. Let me pray, fast, and give alms in secret today. Let me offer them all for the good of others, especially . . ." (Continue in your own words.)

Listen to Jesus.

I love it when you pray for others. Then our hearts beat together. What else is Jesus saying to you?

Ask God to show you how to live today.

"Lord, I start Lent with great hope. Give me grace to persevere one day at a time. Amen."

Thursday, March 2, 2017

Know that God is present with you and ready to converse.

"Jesus, you have the words of eternal life. What must I do to inherit eternal life?"

Read the gospel: Luke 9:22–25.

Jesus said, "The Son of Man must undergo great suffering, and be rejected by the elders, chief priests, and scribes, and be killed, and on the third day be raised."

Then he said to them all, "If any want to become my followers, let them deny themselves and take up their cross daily and follow me. For those who want to save their life will lose it, and those who lose their life for my sake will save it. What does it profit them if they gain the whole world, but lose or forfeit themselves?"

Notice what you think and feel as you read the gospel.

Jesus predicts his passion, death, and resurrection, then urges his followers to take up their own crosses daily. He says if we try to save our lives, we will lose them, but those who lose their lives for his sake will save them.

Pray as you are led for yourself and others.

"Lord, teach me your way of denying myself and losing my life for your sake, for I long for eternal life with you. I give you everything, including . . ." (Continue in your own words.)

Listen to Jesus.

You have nothing to fear, beloved. As long as I am with you, you have everything you need. What else is Jesus saying to you?

Ask God to show you how to live today.

"Put me in situations today, Lord, where I can see my choice of saving or losing my life, and let me choose the way of self-denial, not for my sake but for yours. Amen."

Friday, March 3, 2017

Know that God is present with you and ready to converse.

"Father, Son, and Holy Spirit, one Lord, you are present before me in the Spirit and in the Word. I glorify you."

Read the gospel: Matthew 9:14–15.

Then the disciples of John came to Jesus, saying, "Why do we and the Pharisees fast often, but your disciples do not fast?" And Jesus said to them, "The wedding-guests cannot mourn as long as the bridegroom is with them, can they? The days will come when the bridegroom is taken away from them, and then they will fast."

Notice what you think and feel as you read the gospel.

Jesus answers the question posed to him by the disciples of John: Why don't your disciples fast? Jesus' answer points to who he is: the Messiah, the Bridegroom. As wedding guests, his disciples cannot fast.

Pray as you are led for yourself and others.

"Jesus, you are always with me, yet I long to look upon your face. With that hope, let me rejoice as I fast, developing hunger for your loveliness . . ." (Continue in your own words.)

Listen to Jesus.

I am the Bridegroom who embraces you and loves you, dear one. Ask of me what you will. What else is Jesus saying to you?

Ask God to show you how to live today.

"Lord, I cannot do much in my own strength and discipline. I depend upon your grace. I thank you for it, Lord. Amen."

Saturday, March 4, 2017

**Know that God is present
with you and ready to converse.**

"Lord, Creator of all, you made humans in the image
of God. You know me inside and out. Let me respond
to your call."

Read the gospel: Luke 5:27–32.

After this Jesus went out and saw a tax-collector
named Levi, sitting at the tax booth; and he said to
him, "Follow me." And he got up, left everything, and
followed him.

Then Levi gave a great banquet for him in his
house; and there was a large crowd of tax-collectors
and others sitting at the table with them. The Pharisees
and their scribes were complaining to his disciples,
saying, "Why do you eat and drink with tax-collectors
and sinners?" Jesus answered, "Those who are well
have no need of a physician, but those who are sick;
I have come to call not the righteous but sinners to
repentance."

**Notice what you think
and feel as you read the gospel.**

Jesus must have known Levi's willingness of heart
when he called him, for Levi simply left everything and
followed him immediately. Or did Jesus speak
with such authority that his invitation was irresist-
ible? The way the Pharisees and the scribes grumble

about Jesus' eating with him suggest that they, at least, assume that Levi was a great sinner. Jesus doesn't deny it. He says he came to call sinners, not the righteous, to repentance.

Pray as you are led for yourself and others.

"Lord, I am a sinner. Call me. Levi became Matthew and served you well. What will you make of me?" (Continue in your own words.)

Listen to Jesus.

Beloved, I will make you my lover, more than spouse, friend, sister, or brother. Our work together starts with our love for one another. What else is Jesus saying to you?

Ask God to show you how to live today.

"If I see someone I judge to be a sinner today, let me pray for him or her, knowing that you love that person and call him or her to yourself. Inspire me to speak or act in a loving way toward that person. Amen."

FIRST WEEK OF LENT

O ur pilgrimage on earth cannot be exempt from trial. We progress by means of trial. No one knows himself except through trial, or receives a crown except after victory, or strives except against an enemy or temptation.

St. Augustine
Office of Readings
First Sunday of Lent

Sunday, March 5, 2017
First Sunday of Lent

Know that God is present
with you and ready to converse.

Lent is a season set aside to root out habits of sin in our lives. First we must acknowledge our sins, then we must confess them, and then we must develop strategies to avoid them in the future. We need Jesus to help us in this noble quest. Having been tempted himself, he knows how to help us.

"Lord, here with me now, let me receive your Word, your Spirit, deep into my soul that I may stand in the hour of my temptation."

Read the gospel: Matthew 4:1–11.

Then Jesus was led up by the Spirit into the wilderness to be tempted by the devil. He fasted for forty days and forty nights, and afterwards he was famished. The tempter came and said to him, "If you are the Son of God, command these stones to become loaves of bread." But he answered, "It is written,

'One does not live by bread alone,
    but by every word that comes from the mouth
    of God.'"

Then the devil took him to the holy city and placed him on the pinnacle of the temple, saying to him, "If you are the Son of God, throw yourself down; for it is written,

'He will command his angels concerning you,'
    and 'On their hands they will bear you up,
  so that you will not dash your foot against a stone.'"

Jesus said to him, "Again it is written, 'Do not put the Lord your God to the test.'"

Again, the devil took him to a very high mountain and showed him all the kingdoms of the world and their splendor; and he said to him, "All these I will give you, if you will fall down and worship me." Jesus said to him, "Away with you, Satan! for it is written,

'Worship the Lord your God,
    and serve only him.'"

Then the devil left him, and suddenly angels came and waited on him.

Notice what you think and feel as you read the gospel.

Jesus resists all the temptations of the devil, out-dueling him with scripture. The devil betrays what he himself desires, but Jesus desires only to do the will of his Father. We, too, are to live by every word that proceeds from the mouth of God.

Pray as you are led for yourself and others.

"Lord, I wish to live by your Word. That is why I am praying with today's gospel. In your name, Jesus, give me power over these temptations in my life . . ." (Continue in your own words.)

Listen to Jesus.

I give you power, dear disciple, to do what you cannot do on your own. Receive the Holy Spirit and overcome temptation. What else is Jesus saying to you?

Ask God to show you how to live today.

"Lord, help me to replace sins and temptations with good and lovely things. Let them be my gifts to others. Amen."

Monday, March 6, 2017

Know that God is present with you and ready to converse.

"Lord, I entrust my personal salvation to you. By your Word, help me to serve you and others in my community."

Read the gospel: Matthew 25:31–40 (Mt 25:31–46).

Jesus said, "When the Son of Man comes in his glory, and all the angels with him, then he will sit on the throne of his glory. All the nations will be gathered before him, and he will separate people one from another as a shepherd separates the sheep from the goats, and he will put the sheep at his right hand and the goats at the left. Then the king will say to those at his right hand, 'Come, you that are blessed by my Father, inherit the kingdom prepared for you from the foundation of the world; for I was hungry and you gave me food, I was thirsty and you gave me something to drink, I was a stranger and you welcomed me, I was naked and you gave me clothing, I was sick and you took care of me, I was in prison and you visited me.' Then the righteous will answer him, 'Lord, when was it that we saw you hungry and gave you food, or thirsty and gave you something to drink? And when was it that we saw you a stranger and welcomed you, or naked and gave you clothing? And when was it that we saw you sick or in prison and visited you?' And the king will answer them, 'Truly I tell you, just as you did it to one of the least of these who are members of my family, you did it to me.'"

Notice what you think and feel as you read the gospel.

In Jesus' prophetic judgment of the nations, the Son of Man will commend those peoples who served the poor and needy, for he identifies with them. The Lord of Judgment will condemn those nations who ignored the poor and needy. Ours is the age of redemption and grace. Afterward comes judgment.

Pray as you are led for yourself and others.

"Lord, what can I do to serve you in the hungry, poor, homeless, lost, or lonely? Give me eyes to see you . . ." (Continue in your own words.)

Listen to Jesus.

Your love for me will express itself in service to those who suffer. I will show you opportunities, dear disciple. What else is Jesus saying to you?

Ask God to show you how to live today.

"Lord, open my eyes and my heart to opportunities. Let me see you. Thank you. Amen."

Tuesday, March 7, 2017

Know that God is present with you and ready to converse.

"Lord, teach me to pray."

Read the gospel: Matthew 6:7–15.

Jesus said, "When you are praying, do not heap up empty phrases as the Gentiles do; for they think that they will be heard because of their many words. Do not be like them, for your Father knows what you need before you ask him.

"Pray then in this way:

Our Father in heaven,
  hallowed be your name.
  Your kingdom come.
  Your will be done,
    on earth as it is in heaven.
  Give us this day our daily bread.
  And forgive us our debts,

as we also have forgiven our debtors.
And do not bring us to the time of trial,
but rescue us from the evil one.

For if you forgive others their trespasses, your heavenly Father will also forgive you; but if you do not forgive others, neither will your Father forgive your trespasses."

Notice what you think and feel as you read the gospel.

Jesus' great prayer seems to express priorities in our relationship with God and others. First we glorify the Father, seeking the kingdom, embracing God's will on earth. Then we ask for bread, the necessities of our lives. We ask God's forgiveness and offer our own forgiveness of others' sins against us. Finally, we ask for endurance in the time of trial and rescue from evil.

Pray as you are led for yourself and others.

"Jesus, after you teach the prayer, you point out especially our need to forgive others. As I examine my heart, I forgive these people who have hurt me . . ." (Continue in your own words.)

Listen to Jesus.

The love in your life must often take the form of mercy, my child. Do not judge others. I give you eyes of mercy. What else is Jesus saying to you?

Ask God to show you how to live today.

"Chances are that someone will offend me today, Jesus. Give me grace to forgive that person immediately. Make mercy a habit of my heart. Amen."

Wednesday, March 8, 2017

Know that God is present with you and ready to converse.

"Jesus, no one ever spoke as you did. Speak to me by your Word."

Read the gospel: Luke 11:29–32.

When the crowds were increasing, Jesus began to say, "This generation is an evil generation; it asks for a sign, but no sign will be given to it except the sign of Jonah. For just as Jonah became a sign to the people of Nineveh, so the Son of Man will be to this generation. The queen of the South will rise at the judgment with the people of this generation and condemn them, because she came from the ends of the earth to listen to the wisdom of Solomon, and see, something greater than Solomon is here! The people of Nineveh will rise up at the judgment with this generation and condemn it, because they repented at the proclamation of Jonah, and see, something greater than Jonah is here!"

Notice what you think and feel as you read the gospel.

Jesus deplores those who seek a sign from him. He likens himself to Jonah who preached repentance and spent three days in the belly of a whale before he emerged. He tells them he is greater than Jonah, greater even than Solomon, for he is the Son of God.

Pray as you are led for yourself and others.

"Lord, you are here. Let me repent at your command and listen to your wisdom. I open myself to understand what you are saying to me now . . ." (Continue in your own words.)

Listen to Jesus.

I am, beloved disciple, the Son of the Father. My words have the power to save you. I have some things I want you to do. What else is Jesus saying to you?

Ask God to show you how to live today.

"Although I am a sinner, I give myself to you for forgiveness, cleansing, and service today. Let me please you, Blessed Lord. Amen."

Thursday, March 9, 2017

**Know that God is present
with you and ready to converse.**

"Gracious Father, always near me, let me pray well and
learn by your Word to do your will."

Read the gospel: Matthew 7:7–12.

Jesus said, "Ask, and it will be given to you; search,
and you will find; knock, and the door will be opened
for you. For everyone who asks receives, and everyone
who searches finds, and for everyone who knocks, the
door will be opened. Is there anyone among you who,
if your child asks for bread, will give a stone? Or if the
child asks for a fish, will give a snake? If you then, who
are evil, know how to give good gifts to your children,
how much more will your Father in heaven give good
things to those who ask him!

"In everything do to others as you would have
them do to you; for this is the law and the prophets."

**Notice what you think
and feel as you read the gospel.**

Jesus urges us to ask, search, and knock, requesting
from God what we desire. God will give us only good
things. Our job? To do unto others as we would have
them do to us.

Pray as you are led for yourself and others.

"Lord, focus me on what I may do for others first. Let me do those things and then return to ask you for the good things I need . . ." (Continue in your own words.)

Listen to Jesus.

It is sweet to be in conversation with you, dear one. Through our intimacy, our friendship will grow into everlasting life in the kingdom of my Father. Desire that. Ask for it. What else is Jesus saying to you?

Ask God to show you how to live today.

"Help me to discern between good things and those things that only appear good. Then let me ask for the good things, Lord. Praise your holy name! Amen."

Friday, March 10, 2017

Know that God is present with you and ready to converse.

"Holy Lord, you are just. Teach me by your Word lest I sin against you or my brother or my sister."

Read the gospel: Matthew 5:20–26.

Jesus said, "For I tell you, unless your righteousness exceeds that of the scribes and Pharisees, you will never enter the kingdom of heaven.

"You have heard that it was said to those of ancient times, 'You shall not murder'; and 'whoever murders shall be liable to judgment.' But I say to you that if you are angry with a brother or sister, you will be liable to judgment; and if you insult a brother or sister, you will be liable to the council; and if you say, 'You fool,' you will be liable to the hell of fire. So when you are offering your gift at the altar, if you remember that your brother or sister has something against you, leave your gift there before the altar and go; first be reconciled to your brother or sister, and then come and offer your gift. Come to terms quickly with your accuser while you are on the way to court with him, or your accuser may hand you over to the judge, and the judge to the guard, and you will be thrown into prison. Truly I tell you, you will never get out until you have paid the last penny."

Notice what you think and feel as you read the gospel.

Jesus raises the standard set by Moses's commandments. Anger in the heart is akin to murder and to indulge it is to risk judgment. The solution is to go to a brother or sister who has something against us and reconcile. Jesus asks us to take the initiative even when the other person is angry toward us.

Pray as you are led for yourself and others.

"Lord, who in my life is angry with me, harboring grudges against me, offended by me? Lord, I think of these . . ." (Continue in your own words.)

Listen to Jesus.

I will give you opportunities to reconcile with those with whom you need to reconcile. Be open to these opportunities as there can be healing. What else is Jesus saying to you?

Ask God to show you how to live today.

"My life is complicated, Lord. Sometimes I feel I drag my sins along with me. Help me to have hope and break free by your power. I cannot do it alone, Jesus. Amen."

Saturday, March 11, 2017

Know that God is present with you and ready to converse.

"Jesus, risen Lord, I listen to your Word today. Let me also be a doer of your Word."

Read the gospel: Matthew 5:43–48.

Jesus said, "You have heard that it was said, 'You shall love your neighbor and hate your enemy.' But I say to you, Love your enemies and pray for those who persecute you, so that you may be children of your Father in heaven; for he makes his sun rise on the evil and on the good, and sends rain on the righteous and on the unrighteous. For if you love those who love you, what reward do you have? Do not even the tax-collectors do the same? And if you greet only your brothers and sisters, what more are you doing than others? Do not

even the Gentiles do the same? Be perfect, therefore,
as your heavenly Father is perfect."

Notice what you think
and feel as you read the gospel.

Again Jesus raises the bar of holiness. He calls us to
holiness, the very perfection of the heavenly Father.
The holiness of God requires us to love our enemies
and our persecutors. God does. Jesus wouldn't ask us
to do something impossible.

Pray as you are led for yourself and others.

"Lord, I am far from your holiness, but I open my heart
for your enabling grace. Who is my enemy, who per-
secutes me? These people will I love . . ." (Continue in
your own words.)

Listen to Jesus.

*In humility you learn to love those who oppose you. See
others with the mercy I give you.* What else is Jesus saying
to you?

Ask God to show you how to live today.

"Every day is a new chance to obey your Spirit and
act in love. Prepare me for those moments today. Let
me succeed in loving someone who hates me, hurts
me. Amen."

SECOND WEEK OF LENT

Today, the Second Sunday of Lent, as we continue on the penitential journey, the liturgy invites us, after presenting the Gospel of Jesus' temptations in the desert last week, to reflect on the extraordinary event of the Transfiguration on the mountain. Considered together, these episodes anticipate the Paschal Mystery: Jesus' struggle with the tempter preludes the great final duel of the Passion, while the light of his transfigured Body anticipates the glory of the Resurrection. On the one hand, we see Jesus, fully man, sharing with us even temptation; on the other, we contemplate him as the Son of God who divinizes our humanity. Thus, we could say that these two Sundays serve as pillars on which to build the entire structure of Lent until Easter, and indeed, the entire structure of Christian life, which consists essentially in paschal dynamism: from death to life.

Pope Benedict XVI
February 17, 2008

Sunday, March 12, 2017
Second Sunday of Lent

**Know that God is present
with you and ready to converse.**

Lent is the season in which we focus on moral correction, aligning ourselves with the commandments of Jesus. They are summed up in loving God with all one's might and loving one's neighbor as one's self, but Jesus details what this means in various contexts in the Lenten gospels. He wills to heal our blindness to our sins, especially those habitual sins we rationalize or despair of amending.

"Jesus, you were God among us, and your glory was to die for us. Thank you for being with me now as I read your Word."

Read the gospel: Matthew 17:1–9.

Six days later, Jesus took with him Peter and James and his brother John and led them up a high mountain, by themselves. And he was transfigured before them, and his face shone like the sun, and his clothes became dazzling white. Suddenly there appeared to them Moses and Elijah, talking with him. Then Peter said to Jesus, "Lord, it is good for us to be here; if you wish, I will make three dwellings here, one for you, one for Moses, and one for Elijah." While he was still speaking, suddenly a bright cloud overshadowed them, and from the cloud a voice said, "This is my Son, the Beloved; with him I am well pleased; listen to him!" When the disciples heard this, they fell to the ground and were overcome by fear. But Jesus came and touched them, saying, "Get up and do not be afraid." And when they looked up, they saw no one except Jesus himself alone.

As they were coming down the mountain, Jesus ordered them, "Tell no one about the vision until after the Son of Man has been raised from the dead."

Notice what you think and feel as you read the gospel.

Peter, James, and John are amazed by Jesus' transfiguration before them and his meeting with Moses and Elijah. Then the voice from the cloud proclaims the Father's love for the Son and commands that they "listen to him." Later, Jesus asks them to tell no one until he has been raised from the dead.

Pray as you are led for yourself and others.

"Jesus, your divinity keeps breaking through in the gospels. I believe you are the Son of God, and I put my trust in you. Will you help me do your will?" (Continue in your own words.)

Listen to Jesus.

Lean on my grace, my child, for you are beloved of my Father, too. What else is Jesus saying to you?

Ask God to show you how to live today.

"If I feel your presence with me today, let me praise you and do your will. If I do not feel your presence

today, let me praise you and do your will. You are
Lord! Amen."

Monday, March 13, 2017

Know that God is present
with you and ready to converse.

"Merciful God, I depend on your mercy for repentance,
forgiveness, reinstatement as your child, and sanctification. How shall I proceed?"

Read the gospel: Luke 6:36–38.

Jesus said, "Be merciful, just as your Father is merciful.
    "Do not judge, and you will not be judged; do not
condemn, and you will not be condemned. Forgive,
and you will be forgiven; give, and it will be given to
you. A good measure, pressed down, shaken together,
running over, will be put into your lap; for the measure
you give will be the measure you get back."

Notice what you think
and feel as you read the gospel.

Jesus commands us to be merciful toward others as
God is. He commands us not to judge or condemn so
we will not be condemned. He commands us to forgive
and to give, promising that we will receive more than
we can give.

Pray as you are led for yourself and others.

"Lord, I see faults in others often. I cannot help but judge. Cleanse me of this judgmental mindset. Give me your true mercy for . . ." (Continue in your own words.)

Listen to Jesus.

I love your sincere efforts to be made new and pleasing to God. You must rely on my grace at every step. As you allow me to work holiness in you, I shall work. What else is Jesus saying to you?

Ask God to show you how to live today.

"Lord, help me strive to avoid sin and to do good today. Pick me up when I fall and put me back on your path by your grace. Amen."

Tuesday, March 14, 2017

Know that God is present with you and ready to converse.

"Lord, you are high and lifted up in glory even as you are here with me now. I seek your lesson for me today in your Word."

Read the gospel: Matthew 23:1–12.

Then Jesus said to the crowds and to his disciples, "The scribes and the Pharisees sit on Moses' seat; therefore, do whatever they teach you and follow it; but do not

do as they do, for they do not practice what they teach.
They tie up heavy burdens, hard to bear, and lay them
on the shoulders of others; but they themselves are
unwilling to lift a finger to move them. They do all
their deeds to be seen by others; for they make their
phylacteries broad and their fringes long. They love to
have the place of honor at banquets and the best seats
in the synagogues, and to be greeted with respect in the
market-places, and to have people call them rabbi. But
you are not to be called rabbi, for you have one teacher,
and you are all students. And call no one your father
on earth, for you have one Father—the one in heaven.
Nor are you to be called instructors, for you have one
instructor, the Messiah. The greatest among you will
be your servant. All who exalt themselves will be hum-
bled, and all who humble themselves will be exalted."

Notice what you think
and feel as you read the gospel.

Jesus notices that religious people love to exalt themselves and be honored and respected by those they
command. Jesus turns the crowd's attention to the one
Teacher, the Messiah, and to the one Father, God in
heaven. Only those who humble themselves will be
exalted.

Pray as you are led for yourself and others.

"Only you, Lord, are exalted above all forever—you
who came to serve us and die for us. Humility is not a
pose before you, Lord; it is our only rational response

to who you are. Lord, give me clarity so that I may always know my place as your servant . . ." (Continue in your own words.)

Listen to Jesus.

If you want joy, my child, embrace the role of the servant with all your heart. What else is Jesus saying to you?

Ask God to show you how to live today.

"How may I serve today, Lord? Open my eyes and heart to serving you in others. Thank you for your light, Lord. Amen."

Wednesday, March 15, 2017

Know that God is present
with you and ready to converse.

"Lord, let your Word today take my mind off of me and place it on you. Let me hold you in my heart with gratitude and love."

Read the gospel: Matthew 20:17–28.

While Jesus was going up to Jerusalem, he took the twelve disciples aside by themselves, and said to them on the way, "See, we are going up to Jerusalem, and the Son of Man will be handed over to the chief priests and scribes, and they will condemn him to death; then they will hand him over to the Gentiles to be mocked and flogged and crucified; and on the third day he will be raised."

Then the mother of the sons of Zebedee came to him with her sons, and kneeling before him, she asked a favor of him. And he said to her, "What do you want?" She said to him, "Declare that these two sons of mine will sit, one at your right hand and one at your left, in your kingdom." But Jesus answered, "You do not know what you are asking. Are you able to drink the cup that I am about to drink?" They said to him, "We are able." He said to them, "You will indeed drink my cup, but to sit at my right hand and at my left, this is not mine to grant, but it is for those for whom it has been prepared by my Father."

When the ten heard it, they were angry with the two brothers. But Jesus called them to him and said, "You know that the rulers of the Gentiles lord it over them, and their great ones are tyrants over them. It will not be so among you; but whoever wishes to be great among you must be your servant, and whoever wishes to be first among you must be your slave; just as the Son of Man came not to be served but to serve, and to give his life a ransom for many."

Notice what you think
and feel as you read the gospel.

The disciples don't really hear Jesus' announcement of his coming passion, death, and resurrection in Jerusalem. They are caught up in their own jockeying for honor and authority. Jesus tells them that the one who would be great must be a servant, a slave, just like the Son of Man.

Pray as you are led for yourself and others.

"I give myself to you and to others today, Lord. I want to serve as you served. Guide me . . ." (Continue in your own words.)

Listen to Jesus.

Dearly beloved, I am here to serve you still. You wish to be like me in serving others. I will show you how and give you grace to do it. What else is Jesus saying to you?

Ask God to show you how to live today.

"Lord, first I need a servant's attitude. Then I need opportunities to serve. You will help me! I have a new start every day in your grace. Glory to you, Lord. Amen."

Thursday, March 16, 2017

**Know that God is present
with you and ready to converse.**

"Lord, you intervened in human history to save us from ourselves. Let me respond to your Word in the manner you would have me. Let me learn from you."

Read the gospel: Luke 16:19–31.

Jesus said, "There was a rich man who was dressed in purple and fine linen and who feasted sumptuously every day. And at his gate lay a poor man named Lazarus, covered with sores, who longed to satisfy his

hunger with what fell from the rich man's table; even
the dogs would come and lick his sores. The poor man
died and was carried away by the angels to be with
Abraham. The rich man also died and was buried. In
Hades, where he was being tormented, he looked up
and saw Abraham far away with Lazarus by his side.
He called out, 'Father Abraham, have mercy on me,
and send Lazarus to dip the tip of his finger in water
and cool my tongue; for I am in agony in these flames.'
But Abraham said, 'Child, remember that during your
lifetime you received your good things, and Lazarus
in like manner evil things; but now he is comforted
here, and you are in agony. Besides all this, between
you and us a great chasm has been fixed, so that those
who might want to pass from here to you cannot do
so, and no one can cross from there to us.' He said,
'Then, father, I beg you to send him to my father's
house—for I have five brothers—that he may warn
them, so that they will not also come into this place
of torment.' Abraham replied, 'They have Moses and
the prophets; they should listen to them.' He said, 'No,
father Abraham; but if someone goes to them from the
dead, they will repent.' He said to him, 'If they do not
listen to Moses and the prophets, neither will they be
convinced even if someone rises from the dead.'"

Notice what you think
and feel as you read the gospel.

By this parable Jesus shows how blind the rich can be
to those suffering nearby. Their blindness is a moral

failing for which they will be judged and sentenced at death. The rich man discovers it's too late for him now. Abraham tells him that many who are alive will not repent even if they hear from one who has risen from the dead.

Pray as you are led for yourself and others.

"Lord, many do not believe that you have risen from the dead, and they do not see any need to repent. I pray for mercy, repentance, and conversion for them today, including . . ." (Continue in your own words.)

Listen to Jesus.

Your growth in grace is a progression of belief, faith, conviction, assurance. Ask for deepening in faith, hope, and love. This is the way to joy. What else is Jesus saying to you?

Ask God to show you how to live today.

"As I pray for others, Lord, let me deepen in my understanding of you, that I may be truly useful to you and your works of grace. Amen."

Friday, March 17, 2017

Know that God is present
with you and ready to converse.

"Jesus, sometimes people do not understand you; sometimes they do and yet fail to respond. Let me understand your Word and respond as you would have me respond."

Read the gospel: Matthew 21:33–41 (Mt 21:33–43, 45–46).

Jesus said, "Listen to another parable. There was a landowner who planted a vineyard, put a fence around it, dug a wine press in it, and built a watch-tower. Then he leased it to tenants and went to another country. When the harvest time had come, he sent his slaves to the tenants to collect his produce. But the tenants seized his slaves and beat one, killed another, and stoned another. Again he sent other slaves, more than the first; and they treated them in the same way. Finally he sent his son to them, saying, 'They will respect my son.' But when the tenants saw the son, they said to themselves, 'This is the heir; come, let us kill him and get his inheritance.' So they seized him, threw him out of the vineyard, and killed him. Now when the owner of the vineyard comes, what will he do to those tenants?" They said to him, "He will put those wretches to a miserable death, and lease the vineyard to other tenants who will give him the produce at the harvest time."

Notice what you think and feel as you read the gospel.

In this parable, the tenants wish to exploit the property of the landowner. They reject all emissaries who assert the landowner's claim on the vineyard. When the landowner sends his son, they kill him. Even Jesus' hearers recognize the injustice in that.

Pray as you are led for yourself and others.

"Jesus, you know people so well. You speak so clearly to us about our nature. I come to you asking for a new nature, the one you suffered and died to give me. I ask for . . ." (Continue in your own words.)

Listen to Jesus.

I am pleased to give you what you ask for, beloved disciple. Come to me often with simple sincerity. What else is Jesus saying to you?

Ask God to show you how to live today.

"Jesus, let me work for you today, pleasing you and leaving the results to you. Let me trust in the power of acting in love even if I do not see results. Amen."

Saturday, March 18, 2017

Know that God is present with you and ready to converse.

"Father, your Son proclaimed your mercy and your greatness to the world. Give me a fresh love for you by his Word."

Read the gospel: Luke 15:11–24 (Lk 15:1–3, 11–32).

Then Jesus said, "There was a man who had two sons. The younger of them said to his father, 'Father, give me the share of the property that will belong to me.' So he

divided his property between them. A few days later
the younger son gathered all he had and travelled to a
distant country, and there he squandered his property
in dissolute living. When he had spent everything, a
severe famine took place throughout that country, and
he began to be in need. So he went and hired himself
out to one of the citizens of that country, who sent him
to his fields to feed the pigs. He would gladly have
filled himself with the pods that the pigs were eating;
and no one gave him anything. But when he came to
himself he said, 'How many of my father's hired hands
have bread enough and to spare, but here I am dying
of hunger! I will get up and go to my father, and I will
say to him, "Father, I have sinned against heaven and
before you; I am no longer worthy to be called your
son; treat me like one of your hired hands."' So he set
off and went to his father. But while he was still far
off, his father saw him and was filled with compas-
sion; he ran and put his arms around him and kissed
him. Then the son said to him, 'Father, I have sinned
against heaven and before you; I am no longer worthy
to be called your son.' But the father said to his slaves,
'Quickly, bring out a robe—the best one—and put it on
him; put a ring on his finger and sandals on his feet.
And get the fatted calf and kill it, and let us eat and
celebrate; for this son of mine was dead and is alive
again; he was lost and is found!' And they began to
celebrate."

Notice what you think and feel as you read the gospel.

In this great parable, the younger son does something young people have always done: leave home to waste time and money in self-indulgence. When he finds misery instead of freedom and pleasure, he returns repentant to his father, who welcomes him with joy.

Pray as you are led for yourself and others.

"Lord, I am a sinner, craving your mercy and love. I am aware that I deserve neither. How many ways can I praise you?" (Continue in your own words.)

Listen to Jesus.

God is always good—do not forget it. Let God's mercy draw you back home. What else is Jesus saying to you?

Ask God to show you how to live today.

"Thank you for your mercy to me, Lord. Let me never forget how you have lifted me out of selfishness to depend on you and serve you all the days of my life. Amen."

THIRD WEEK OF LENT

Today's gospel presents Jesus' encounter with the Samaritan woman in Sicar, near an old well where the woman went to draw water daily. That day, she found Jesus seated, "wearied as he was with his journey" (Jn 4:6). He immediately says to her: "Give me a drink" (v. 7). . . . This simple request from Jesus is the start of a frank dialogue, through which he enters with great delicacy into the interior world of a person to whom, according to social norms, he should not have spoken. But Jesus does! Jesus is not afraid. When Jesus sees a person he goes ahead, because he loves. He loves us all. He never hesitates before a person out of prejudice. Jesus sets her own situation before her, not by judging her but by making her feel worthy, acknowledged, and thus arousing in her the desire to go beyond the daily routine.

Pope Francis
March 23, 2014

Sunday, March 19, 2017
Third Sunday of Lent

**Know that God is present
with you and ready to converse.**

Jesus, the One sent to reconcile us to the God, had natural parents and grew up in a natural family. This Holy Family now includes all who believe in the Christ. Our Father has a hand on us, shepherding us through our lives, always providing for us what is good, even if we don't always understand it as such. What a privilege to be a child of the Most High God, a brother or sister to our Lord Jesus Christ!

"Jesus, you bought me with your blood. Quench my thirst for you by your Word."

**Read the gospel: John
4:5–26, 39–42 (Jn 4:5–42).**

So Jesus came to a Samaritan city called Sychar, near the plot of ground that Jacob had given to his son Joseph. Jacob's well was there, and Jesus, tired out by his journey, was sitting by the well. It was about noon.

A Samaritan woman came to draw water, and Jesus said to her, "Give me a drink." (His disciples had gone to the city to buy food.) The Samaritan woman said to him, "How is it that you, a Jew, ask a drink of me, a woman of Samaria?" (Jews do not share things in common with Samaritans.) Jesus answered her, "If you knew the gift of God, and who it is that is saying to you, 'Give me a drink,' you would have asked him, and he would have given you living water." The woman said to him, "Sir, you have no bucket, and the well is deep. Where do you get that living water? Are you greater than our ancestor Jacob, who gave us the well, and with his sons and his flocks drank from it?" Jesus said to her, "Everyone who drinks of this water will be thirsty again, but those who drink of the water that I will give them will never be thirsty. The water that I will give will become in them a spring of water gushing up to eternal life." The woman said to him, "Sir, give me this water, so that I may never be thirsty or have to keep coming here to draw water."

Jesus said to her, "Go, call your husband, and come back." The woman answered him, "I have no husband." Jesus said to her, "You are right in saying, 'I have no husband'; for you have had five husbands, and the one you have now is not your husband. What you have said is true!" The woman said to him, "Sir, I see that you are a prophet. Our ancestors worshipped on this mountain, but you say that the place where people must worship is in Jerusalem." Jesus said to her, "Woman, believe me, the hour is coming when you will worship the Father neither on this mountain nor in Jerusalem. You worship what you do not know; we worship what we know, for salvation is from the Jews. But the hour is coming, and is now here, when the true worshippers will worship the Father in spirit and truth, for the Father seeks such as these to worship him. God is spirit, and those who worship him must worship in spirit and truth." The woman said to him, "I know that Messiah is coming (who is called Christ). When he comes, he will proclaim all things to us." Jesus said to her, "I am he, the one who is speaking to you." . . .

Many Samaritans from that city believed in him because of the woman's testimony, "He told me everything I have ever done." So when the Samaritans came to him, they asked him to stay with them; and he stayed there for two days. And many more believed because of his word. They said to the woman, "It is no longer because of what you said that we believe, for we have heard for ourselves, and we know that this is truly the Savior of the world."

Notice what you think and feel as you read the gospel.

Jesus lays aside all religious and cultural rules to speak to the Samaritan woman. It's all about water, developed as a symbol of eternal life. The woman is suspicious, but she is convinced because Jesus knows her past. She departs to tell the village that she may have found the Messiah.

Pray as you are led for yourself and others.

"Lord, I do not deserve a spring in me gushing up to eternal life, but you offer it to those who believe. Jesus, I believe. Let your waters flow through me to others . . ." (Continue in your own words.)

Listen to Jesus.

See, my child, it is not in yourself you find life but in me. Worship God from the depths of your heart and soul, and you will live forever. What else is Jesus saying to you?

Ask God to show you how to live today.

"Lord, I do not always recognize when I am worshipping you in Spirit and in truth. Help me to do so. Help me to worship you often today and all my life. Amen."

Monday, March 20, 2017
Saint Joseph, Spouse
of the Blessed Virgin Mary

Know that God is present
with you and ready to converse.

"Lord, your ways are so high above my ways. Let me be guided, not by my own understanding, but by your Word and your Spirit."

Read the gospel: Matthew 1:16, 18–21, 24.

Joseph the husband of Mary, of whom Jesus was born, who is called the Messiah. . . .

Now the birth of Jesus the Messiah took place in this way. When his mother Mary had been engaged to Joseph, but before they lived together, she was found to be with child from the Holy Spirit. Her husband Joseph, being a righteous man and unwilling to expose her to public disgrace, planned to dismiss her quietly. But just when he had resolved to do this, an angel of the Lord appeared to him in a dream and said, "Joseph, son of David, do not be afraid to take Mary as your wife, for the child conceived in her is from the Holy Spirit. She will bear a son, and you are to name him Jesus, for he will save his people from their sins." . . . When Joseph awoke from sleep, he did as the angel of the Lord commanded him; he took her as his wife.

Notice what you think and feel as you read the gospel.

Joseph needs divine guidance to change his reasonable and compassionate plans about Mary, now pregnant by the Holy Spirit. It takes an angel to convince him of that and to take Mary as his wife despite her pregnancy with a child not his own. The child, he is told, will save the people from their sins.

Pray as you are led for yourself and others.

"St. Joseph, guardian of the Child Jesus and his Mother, the Blessed Virgin Mary, pray for me and help me be a loving child in the Holy Family and a faithful member of the Church, the Body of Christ, which you protect by your intercession. I pray also for those in my family . . ." (Continue in your own words.)

Listen to Jesus.

Stronger than the family of blood is the family of the Spirit, beloved disciple. I have won you a place at the table of the family of God. What else is Jesus saying to you?

Ask God to show you how to live today.

"As a child of God, let me live today as a child—believing, trusting, giving myself for the good of others. Amen."

Tuesday, March 21, 2017

**Know that God is present
with you and ready to converse.**

"Father, let me eat the food your Son, Jesus Christ, gives to me. He is the Word, and he feeds me with himself."

**Read the gospel:
John 4:7–10, 27–42 (Jn 4:5–42).**

A Samaritan woman came to draw water, and Jesus said to her, "Give me a drink." (His disciples had gone to the city to buy food.) The Samaritan woman said to him, "How is it that you, a Jew, ask a drink of me, a woman of Samaria?" (Jews do not share things in common with Samaritans.) Jesus answered her, "If you knew the gift of God, and who it is that is saying to you, 'Give me a drink,' you would have asked him, and he would have given you living water." . . .

Just then his disciples came. They were astonished that he was speaking with a woman, but no one said, "What do you want?" or, "Why are you speaking with her?" Then the woman left her water-jar and went back to the city. She said to the people, "Come and see a man who told me everything I have ever done! He cannot be the Messiah, can he?" They left the city and were on their way to him.

Meanwhile the disciples were urging him, "Rabbi, eat something." But he said to them, "I have food to eat that you do not know about." So the disciples said to one another, "Surely no one has brought him something to eat?" Jesus said to them, "My food is to do the will of him who sent me and to complete his work. Do you not say, 'Four months more, then comes the harvest'? But I tell you, look around you, and see how the fields are ripe for harvesting. The reaper is already receiving wages and is gathering fruit for eternal life, so that sower and reaper may rejoice together. For here the saying holds true, 'One sows and another reaps.' I sent you to reap that for which you did not labor. Others have labored, and you have entered into their labor."

Many Samaritans from that city believed in him because of the woman's testimony, "He told me everything I have ever done." So when the Samaritans came to him, they asked him to stay with them; and he stayed there for two days. And many more believed because of his word. They said to the woman, "It is no longer because of what you said that we believe, for we have heard for ourselves, and we know that this is truly the Savior of the world."

Notice what you think and feel as you read the gospel.

While the disciples go to find food in the Samaritan village, Jesus speaks to the woman at the well outside of town. He turns her life upside down. The disciples return astonished he is speaking with her but don't dare ask about it. When they offer him food, Jesus tells them that his food is to do the will of God, which is to announce the kingdom. The woman and many Samaritans come to believe in him.

Pray as you are led for yourself and others.

"Lord, I pray for both the living water and the food of God. Let me believe and do God's will. Help me see and do God's will in these matters . . ." (Continue in your own words.)

Listen to Jesus.

This is the journey of faith, dear disciple. Entrust yourself entirely to God, giving up your own will and seeking God's. God will work in your life and bless you. What else is Jesus saying to you?

Ask God to show you how to live today.

"Lord, I abandon all to you today. Take all of me and do with me what you will. I seek your power to do what pleases you. Amen."

Wednesday, March 22, 2017

Know that God is present
with you and ready to converse.

"Lord, give me deep understanding of your commandments by your Word. You are present now to teach me by the Word of your Son."

Read the gospel: Matthew 5:17–19.

Jesus said, "Do not think that I have come to abolish the law or the prophets; I have come not to abolish but to fulfill. For truly I tell you, until heaven and earth pass away, not one letter, not one stroke of a letter, will pass from the law until all is accomplished. Therefore, whoever breaks one of the least of these commandments, and teaches others to do the same, will be called least in the kingdom of heaven; but whoever does them and teaches them will be called great in the kingdom of heaven."

Notice what you think
and feel as you read the gospel.

Jesus says he fulfills the law and the prophets, and all they have said will come to pass. Those who break their commandments will be called least in the kingdom, especially those who teach others to break them.

Pray as you are led for yourself and others.

"Lord, let me not abuse the liberty of your law of love, which comprises all of the law and the prophets. Let me understand deeply that God's morality is exacting, and I am called to obedience, not for the sake of legality but for the sake of love. Keep me from leading any of these into error . . ." (Continue in your own words.)

Listen to Jesus.

The proper fear of God is to guard yourself and your heart that you may not offend God. If you sin, you may come to the infinite forgiveness I offer. I will wash you white as snow. What else is Jesus saying to you?

Ask God to show you how to live today.

"Lord, I place my sinful self in your hands. Only you can forgive and cleanse me. Give me your Spirit that I may walk in your grace and reflect your grace upon others. Amen."

Thursday, March 23, 2017

Know that God is present with you and ready to converse.

"Lord, I live in a world full of spiritual forces. I seek only you by the Holy Spirit. Let the Spirit illuminate your Word to me."

Read the gospel: Luke 11:14–23.

Now Jesus was casting out a demon that was mute; when the demon had gone out, the one who had been mute spoke, and the crowds were amazed. But some of them said, "He casts out demons by Beelzebul, the ruler of the demons." Others, to test him, kept demanding from him a sign from heaven. But he knew what they were thinking and said to them, "Every kingdom divided against itself becomes a desert, and house falls on house. If Satan also is divided against himself, how will his kingdom stand?—for you say that I cast out the demons by Beelzebul. Now if I cast out the demons by Beelzebul, by whom do your exorcists cast them out? Therefore they will be your judges. But if it is by the finger of God that I cast out the demons, then the kingdom of God has come to you. When a strong man, fully armed, guards his castle, his property is safe. But when one stronger than he attacks him and overpowers him, he takes away his armor in which he trusted and divides his plunder. Whoever is not with me is against me, and whoever does not gather with me scatters."

Notice what you think and feel as you read the gospel.

Seeing his power over evil spirits, some in the crowd accuse Jesus of being in league with Satan, Beelzebul. Jesus repudiates that idea, pointing out that a divided kingdom cannot stand. He describes himself as a man stronger than the strong man for he exercises the power of God.

Pray as you are led for yourself and others.

"Lord, protect me and those I love from evil. Vanquish evil by your power, and let us all gather with you . . ." (Continue in your own words.)

Listen to Jesus.

Dearest soul, I am your protector. Sometimes you will be opposed by powers greater than yourself. Always turn to me, trusting me and praying for my protection, for there is no power greater than I. What else is Jesus saying to you?

Ask God to show you how to live today.

"Lord, if there is any evil jeopardizing me or those you have given me, direct me to pray. Give me discernment that I may turn to you for all rescue and protection. Thank you, mighty Savior. Amen."

Friday, March 24, 2017

**Know that God is present
with you and ready to converse.**

"Lord, I am here before you, hungry for your Word."

Read the gospel: Mark 12:28–34.

One of the scribes came near and heard them disputing with one another, and seeing that Jesus answered them well, he asked Jesus, "Which commandment is the first of all?" Jesus answered, "The first is, 'Hear, O Israel: the Lord our God, the Lord is one; you shall

love the Lord your God with all your heart, and with
all your soul, and with all your mind, and with all
your strength.' The second is this, 'You shall love your
neighbor as yourself.' There is no other commandment
greater than these." Then the scribe said to him, "You
are right, Teacher; you have truly said that 'he is one,
and besides him there is no other'; and 'to love him
with all the heart, and with all the understanding, and
with all the strength,' and 'to love one's neighbor as
oneself,'—this is much more important than all whole
burnt-offerings and sacrifices." When Jesus saw that
he answered wisely, he said to him, "You are not far
from the kingdom of God." After that no one dared to
ask him any question.

Notice what you think
and feel as you read the gospel.

Jesus must have loved the scribe who understood the
greatest commandments of the law. Loving God and
one's neighbor includes all the commandments of the
law and the prophets. Jesus assures the scribe he is "not
far" from the kingdom.

Pray as you are led for yourself and others.

"Lord, I embrace your law of love. Fill me with the love
in your own heart. Let me love others as you loved the
scribe . . ." (Continue in your own words.)

Listen to Jesus.

In love is all your power, dear disciple. Take up your cross and follow me in your journey of love. What else is Jesus saying to you?

Ask God to show you how to live today.

"Lord, if you walk with me, I can bear my cross today. Fill me with love for others so that I may love with your love. I glorify your name, blessed Savior. Amen."

Saturday, March 25, 2017
Annunciation of the Lord

**Know that God is present
with you and ready to converse.**

"Here am I before you, Lord God of Hosts. Teach me by your Word to do your will."

Read the gospel: Luke 1:26–38.

In the sixth month the angel Gabriel was sent by God to a town in Galilee called Nazareth, to a virgin engaged to a man whose name was Joseph, of the house of David. The virgin's name was Mary. And he came to her and said, "Greetings, favored one! The Lord is with you." But she was much perplexed by his words and pondered what sort of greeting this might be. The angel said to her, "Do not be afraid, Mary, for you have found favor with God. And now, you will conceive in your womb and bear a son, and you will

name him Jesus. He will be great, and will be called
the Son of the Most High, and the Lord God will give
to him the throne of his ancestor David. He will reign
over the house of Jacob forever, and of his kingdom
there will be no end." Mary said to the angel, "How
can this be, since I am a virgin?" The angel said to her,
"The Holy Spirit will come upon you, and the power
of the Most High will overshadow you; therefore the
child to be born will be holy; he will be called Son of
God. And now, your relative Elizabeth in her old age
has also conceived a son; and this is the sixth month
for her who was said to be barren. For nothing will be
impossible with God." Then Mary said, "Here am I, the
servant of the Lord; let it be with me according to your
word." Then the angel departed from her.

Notice what you think and feel as you read the gospel.

Usually in scripture people who see angels are stricken
with fear. Not so Mary, a young teenager dedicated to
God. Mary is not afraid of the angel, but she is perplexed by the greeting and by the prophetic message
that she would be the Mother of the Son of the Most
High God. But her spirit was open and she said yes to
the Holy Spirit.

Pray as you are led for yourself and others.

"Mary, I honor you for your willingness to be the
Mother of God. I bless you. I ask your prayers, Mother,
for these . . ." (Continue in your own words.)

Listen to Jesus.

I love my Mother, too, and honor her as you do. She prays for you and all her children. God hears her. What else is Jesus saying to you?

Ask God to show you how to live today.

"Lord, by your grace help me to say yes to your will today. Show me that nothing is impossible with God. Amen."

FOURTH WEEK OF LENT

Joy and light are the dominant theme of today's liturgy. The gospel narrates the story of "a man born blind" (Jn 9:1). . . . The man born blind represents the human person marred by sin who desires to know the truth about himself and his personal destiny but is prevented from doing so by congenital illness. Only Jesus can cure him: He is "the light of the world" (Jn 9:5). Handing himself over to him, every human being who is spiritually blind from birth has the fresh possibility of "coming to the light," namely to supernatural life.

St. John Paul II
March 10, 2002

Sunday, March 26, 2017
Fourth Sunday of Lent

**Know that God is present
with you and ready to converse.**

In this week of Lent, the gospels show Jesus at work,
healing and preaching. The disputes against him are
getting more intense as the scribes and Pharisees get
a clearer understanding that he is claiming that God
is his Father and that they are one. Jesus encounters
blindness in many forms on his way to the Cross.

"Lord, open my eyes that I may see you in your
holy Word."

**Read the gospel:
John 9:1–7, 13–17, 39–41 (Jn 9:1–41).**

As Jesus walked along, he saw a man blind from
birth. His disciples asked him, "Rabbi, who sinned,
this man or his parents, that he was born blind?" Jesus
answered, "Neither this man nor his parents sinned; he
was born blind so that God's works might be revealed
in him. We must work the works of him who sent me
while it is day; night is coming when no one can work.
As long as I am in the world, I am the light of the
world." When he had said this, he spat on the ground
and made mud with the saliva and spread the mud
on the man's eyes, saying to him, "Go, wash in the
pool of Siloam" (which means Sent). Then he went and
washed and came back able to see. . . .

They brought to the Pharisees the man who had formerly been blind. Now it was a sabbath day when Jesus made the mud and opened his eyes. Then the Pharisees also began to ask him how he had received his sight. He said to them, "He put mud on my eyes. Then I washed, and now I see." Some of the Pharisees said, "This man is not from God, for he does not observe the sabbath." But others said, "How can a man who is a sinner perform such signs?" And they were divided. So they said again to the blind man, "What do you say about him? It was your eyes he opened." He said, "He is a prophet." . . .

Jesus said, "I came into this world for judgement so that those who do not see may see, and those who do see may become blind." Some of the Pharisees near him heard this and said to him, "Surely we are not blind, are we?" Jesus said to them, "If you were blind, you would not have sin. But now that you say, 'We see,' your sin remains."

Notice what you think and feel as you read the gospel.

The disciples ask Jesus who has sinned that a man is born blind. Jesus says it is not about sin but about revealing the glory of God. Then he heals the blind man. The Pharisees interrogate the man who had been blind, and when they hear his story they deny that Jesus could be from God. Jesus says that those who think they see but deny him are blind.

Pray as you are led for yourself and others.

"Lord, I cannot pretend to see. I long to see your face. Heal me deep within, and heal those you have given me . . ." (Continue in your own words.)

Listen to Jesus.

It is my joy to open your heart, mind, and soul to me, my child. Give yourself to me every day, and I will change your life. What else is Jesus saying to you?

Ask God to show you how to live today.

"Lead me by the hand, Lord. Lead me into your light. And let me do something that pleases you today. Amen."

Monday, March 27, 2017

**Know that God is present
with you and ready to converse.**

"Lord, let me find you in the darkness of the world and even within my own darkness. You are the Light of the World."

**Read the gospel:
John 9:13–16, 18–21, 24–38 (Jn 9:1–41).**

They brought to the Pharisees the man who had formerly been blind. Now it was a sabbath day when Jesus made the mud and opened his eyes. Then the Pharisees also began to ask him how he had received his sight. He said to them, "He put mud on my eyes. Then I washed, and now I see." Some of the Pharisees said, "This man is not from God, for he does not observe the sabbath." But others said, "How can a man who is a sinner perform such signs?" And they were divided. . . .

The Jews did not believe that he had been blind and had received his sight until they called the parents of the man who had received his sight and asked them, "Is this your son, who you say was born blind? How then does he now see?" His parents answered, "We know that this is our son, and that he was born blind; but we do not know how it is that now he sees, nor do we know who opened his eyes. Ask him; he is of age. He will speak for himself." . . .

So for the second time they called the man who had been blind, and they said to him, "Give glory to God! We know that this man is a sinner." He answered, "I do not know whether he is a sinner. One thing I do know, that though I was blind, now I see." They said to him, "What did he do to you? How did he open your eyes?" He answered them, "I have told you already, and you would not listen. Why do you want to hear it again? Do you also want to become his disciples?" Then they reviled him, saying, "You are his disciple, but we are disciples of Moses. We know that God has spoken to Moses, but as for this man, we do not know where he comes from." The man answered, "Here is an astonishing thing! You do not know where he comes from, and yet he opened my eyes. We know that God does not listen to sinners, but he does listen to one who worships him and obeys his will. Never since the world began has it been heard that anyone opened the eyes of a person born blind. If this man were not from God, he could do nothing." They answered him, "You were born entirely in sins, and are you trying to teach us?" And they drove him out.

Jesus heard that they had driven him out, and when he found him, he said, "Do you believe in the Son of Man?" He answered, "And who is he, sir? Tell me, so that I may believe in him." Jesus said to him, "You have seen him, and the one speaking with you is he." He said, "Lord, I believe." And he worshipped him.

Notice what you think and feel as you read the gospel.

This passage is a study of human nature. All are in the dark whether they realize it or not. The disciples don't understand. The blind man doesn't see anything. His parents can't explain his healing. The Pharisees cannot see past the fact that Jesus breaks the Sabbath according to their laws. They are blinded by their theology. Meanwhile, the man restored to sight believes in Jesus, the Messiah.

Pray as you are led for yourself and others.

"Lord, though all the world be wrong, you are right. I believe in you and worship you. As we have a personal relationship, I pray the same for others, especially those in deepest darkness . . ." (Continue in your own words.)

Listen to Jesus.

I cannot do my work in those who deny their sins, beloved disciple. Give all your sins to me and let me wash you. You will know my joy. What else is Jesus saying to you?

Ask God to show you how to live today.

"What sacrifice can I make today to show my love for you, my gratitude that you are with me, Savior? Amen."

Tuesday, March 28, 2017

Know that God is present
with you and ready to converse.

"Lord of heaven and earth, stir up my heart to receive your Word today."

Read the gospel: John
5:1–9a, 14–16 (Jn 5:1–16).

After this there was a festival of the Jews, and Jesus went up to Jerusalem.

Now in Jerusalem by the Sheep Gate there is a pool, called in Hebrew Beth-zatha, which has five porticoes. In these lay many invalids—blind, lame, and paralyzed. One man was there who had been ill for thirty-eight years. When Jesus saw him lying there and knew that he had been there a long time, he said to him, "Do you want to be made well?" The sick man answered him, "Sir, I have no one to put me into the pool when the water is stirred up; and while I am making my way, someone else steps down ahead of me." Jesus said to him, "Stand up, take your mat and walk." At once the man was made well, and he took up his mat and began to walk. . . .

Later Jesus found him in the temple and said to him, "See, you have been made well! Do not sin anymore, so that nothing worse happens to you." The man went away and told the Jews that it was Jesus who had made him well. Therefore the Jews started persecuting Jesus, because he was doing such things on the sabbath.

Notice what you think and feel as you read the gospel.

On this Sabbath, Jesus tells the paralyzed man to take up his mat and walk, and he does so. Some Jews tell the man that it is unlawful for him to carry his mat on the Sabbath. These Jews started persecuting Jesus for healing on the Sabbath.

Pray as you are led for yourself and others.

"How narrow is the human heart, Lord! How easily we reject your free ways of love and allow ourselves to be imprisoned by human rules and expectations. Free us from this sin . . ." (Continue in your own words.)

Listen to Jesus.

If you offer yourself to act upon my love, you, too, will meet opposition. But I will be with you, and I will work through you, dear disciple. What else is Jesus saying to you?

Ask God to show you how to live today.

"Lord, all I ask is to walk in your grace, following you, doing small acts of love. Amen."

Wednesday, March 29, 2017

**Know that God is present
with you and ready to converse.**

"Father, in the unity of the Holy Spirit you are one with your Son, Jesus, who is the everlasting Word. Let me join you in your love."

Read the gospel: John 5:17–24 (Jn 5:17–30).

But Jesus answered them, "My Father is still working, and I also am working." For this reason the Jews were seeking all the more to kill him, because he was not only breaking the sabbath, but was also calling God his own Father, thereby making himself equal to God.

Jesus said to them, "Very truly, I tell you, the Son can do nothing on his own, but only what he sees the Father doing; for whatever the Father does, the Son does likewise. The Father loves the Son and shows him all that he himself is doing; and he will show him greater works than these, so that you will be astonished. Indeed, just as the Father raises the dead and gives them life, so also the Son gives life to whomsoever he wishes. The Father judges no one but has given all judgment to the Son, so that all may honor the Son just as they honor the Father. Anyone who does not honor the Son does not honor the Father who sent him. Very truly, I tell you, anyone who hears my word and believes him who sent me has eternal life, and does not come under judgment, but has passed from death to life."

Notice what you think and feel as you read the gospel.

Some of the Jews want to kill Jesus now not just because he breaks the Sabbath but even more because he makes himself equal to God by healing, forgiving, raising the dead, and proclaiming that in the end he will judge all humanity. He and the Father are one; he does only the Father's will.

Pray as you are led for yourself and others.

"I can imagine how stunned people were to hear your words, Lord. You spoke the truth, but it was too much for many to take in. Open my spirit to humility to receive and believe the truth, your perfect unity with the Father, your life-giving authority . . ." (Continue in your own words.)

Listen to Jesus.

My work of redemption is a complete work, still in process. I did not come to give temporary relief to a fallen race; I came to raise all who trust in me to eternal life with God. Let me work in you, beloved. What else is Jesus saying to you?

Ask God to show you how to live today.

"Jesus, make your saving power real in me. Let me extend it by your grace and guidance to someone else today. I am grateful to you, blessed Lord. Amen."

Thursday, March 30, 2017

Know that God is present with you and ready to converse.

"Word of God, Savior, Jesus, let me hear you and know your voice today."

Read the gospel: John 5:31–38 (Jn 5:31–47).

Jesus said, "If I testify about myself, my testimony is not true. There is another who testifies on my behalf, and I know that his testimony to me is true. You sent messengers to John, and he testified to the truth. Not that I accept such human testimony, but I say these things so that you may be saved. He was a burning and shining lamp, and you were willing to rejoice for a while in his light. But I have a testimony greater than John's. The works that the Father has given me to complete, the very works that I am doing, testify on my behalf that the Father has sent me. And the Father who sent me has himself testified on my behalf. You have never heard his voice or seen his form, and you do not have his word abiding in you, because you do not believe him whom he has sent."

Notice what you think and feel as you read the gospel.

Jesus points out the things that testify to him as the Messiah. These are not his own testimony, but God's, he says. John the Baptist, the mighty works Jesus did, and the scriptures all testify to Jesus as the Messiah. But many who hear him do not believe because they do not have the love of God in them.

Pray as you are led for yourself and others.

"Lord, how can I keep the love of God within myself and share it with others? I need your grace, and I pray you give grace to these you have given me . . ." (Continue in your own words.)

Listen to Jesus.

Beloved, I have made life easy for you: merely love me. As long as you love me, we journey together, you are safe, you can do God's will, and your prayers are powerful. What else is Jesus saying to you?

Ask God to show you how to live today.

"Lord, increase my love of God and neighbor, that I may bring glory to you. Thank you! Amen."

Friday, March 31, 2017

**Know that God is present
with you and ready to converse.**

"One God, I am before you, in awe at your wonderful works in the universe, in history, in the salvation of your people. Teach me by your Word."

Read the gospel: John 7:1–2, 10, 25–30.

After this Jesus went about in Galilee. He did not wish to go about in Judea because the Jews were looking for an opportunity to kill him. Now the Jewish festival of Booths was near. . . .

But after his brothers had gone to the festival, then he also went, not publicly but as it were in secret. . . .

Now some of the people of Jerusalem were saying, "Is not this the man whom they are trying to kill? And here he is, speaking openly, but they say nothing to him! Can it be that the authorities really know that this is the Messiah? Yet we know where this man is from; but when the Messiah comes, no one will know where he is from." Then Jesus cried out as he was teaching in the temple, "You know me, and you know where I am from. I have not come on my own. But the one who sent me is true, and you do not know him. I know him, because I am from him, and he sent me." Then they tried to arrest him, but no one laid hands on him, because his hour had not yet come.

Notice what you think and feel as you read the gospel.

In Jerusalem now, Jesus is in great danger. He moves about in secret. Meanwhile, people of Jerusalem speculate about his being the Messiah. Others argue against that idea. Jesus now cries out in the temple that he has been sent by God, whom they do not know. They try but fail to arrest him for his hour had not yet come.

Pray as you are led for yourself and others.

"Lord, I, too, give myself to your timing and the events you have destined in my life. Let me be true to you and embrace your will. Let it be for the good of others . . ." (Continue in your own words.)

Listen to Jesus.

It was my glory to be crucified in shame before men and women. I did it for love. My Cross is also your glory, dear disciple. Take up your own cross in love and follow me to glory. What else is Jesus saying to you?

Ask God to show you how to live today.

"Let me make a small or great sacrifice in love today, Lord. Let it be to glorify you. I praise the way of the cross, Jesus. Thank you for teaching me. Amen."

Saturday, April 1, 2017

Know that God is present
with you and ready to converse.

"Lord, as I come into your presence, let all doubt and
disputation die in me, and let me receive the truth of
your Word."

Read the gospel: John 7:40–53.

When they heard Jesus' words, some in the crowd said,
"This is really the prophet." Others said, "This is the
Messiah." But some asked, "Surely the Messiah does
not come from Galilee, does he? Has not the scripture said that the Messiah is descended from David
and comes from Bethlehem, the village where David
lived?" So there was a division in the crowd because
of him. Some of them wanted to arrest him, but no one
laid hands on him.

Then the temple police went back to the chief
priests and Pharisees, who asked them, "Why did
you not arrest him?" The police answered, "Never has
anyone spoken like this!" Then the Pharisees replied,
"Surely you have not been deceived too, have you?
Has any one of the authorities or of the Pharisees
believed in him? But this crowd, which does not know
the law—they are accursed." Nicodemus, who had
gone to Jesus before, and who was one of them, asked,
"Our law does not judge people without first giving
them a hearing to find out what they are doing, does
it?" They replied, "Surely you are not also from Galilee,

are you? Search and you will see that no prophet is to
arise from Galilee."

Then each of them went home.

Notice what you think
and feel as you read the gospel.

The people of Jerusalem are arguing about Jesus. They
speak from partial knowledge, and they form their
opinions based on self-interest, not regard for the truth.
The Pharisees condemn the crowd's ignorance of the
law, but Nicodemus points out that they themselves
unfairly judge Jesus contrary to the law.

Pray as you are led for yourself and others.

"Lord, I can get swept into confusion by all the argu-
ments of my own day. My knowledge is partial, my
prejudices hold sway, and I am distracted from having a pure encounter with you. Let me know you and
worship you with all my heart . . ." (Continue in your
own words.)

Listen to Jesus.

*My beloved servant, I give you my heart as you have given me
yours. By faith you see me, by love you know me. What else
do you ask of me today?* What else is Jesus saying to you?

Ask God to show you how to live today.

"Thank you for your wonderful love for me, Lord. Let
nothing ever come between us. I humbly ask that I may
radiate your love to others today. Amen."

FIFTH WEEK OF LENT

Before the sealed tomb of his friend Lazarus, Jesus "cried with a loud voice: 'Lazarus, come out!' And the dead man came out, his hands and feet bound with bandages, and his face wrapped with a cloth" (Jn 11:43–44). This cry is an imperative to all men because we are all marked by death, all of us. . . . Christ is not resigned to the tombs that we have built for ourselves with our choice for evil and death, with our errors, with our sins. He is not resigned to this! He invites us, almost orders us, to come out of the tomb in which our sins have buried us. He calls us insistently to come out of the darkness of that prison in which we are enclosed, content with a false, selfish and mediocre life. "Come out!" he says to us, "Come out!"

Pope Francis
April 6, 2014

Sunday, April 2, 2017
Fifth Sunday of Lent

Know that God is present
with you and ready to converse.

Lent continues with gospels showing intensifying opposition to Jesus who, for his part, continues to work great miracles and speak more and more plainly even to those who wish to kill him. He shows no fear for he walks in the light of his Father and he wholly trusts the providence of God. Though he journeys toward his death, he has come to bring life.

"Jesus, you who began my salvation, I ask you to finish it according to your will. Let me follow you in your Word."

Read the gospel:
John 11:1–6, 38–45 (Jn 11:1–45).

Now a certain man was ill, Lazarus of Bethany, the village of Mary and her sister Martha. Mary was the one who anointed the Lord with perfume and wiped his feet with her hair; her brother Lazarus was ill. So the sisters sent a message to Jesus, "Lord, he whom you love is ill." But when Jesus heard it, he said, "This illness does not lead to death; rather it is for God's glory, so that the Son of God may be glorified through it." Accordingly, though Jesus loved Martha and her sister and Lazarus, after having heard that Lazarus was ill, he stayed two days longer in the place where he was. . . .

Then Jesus, again greatly disturbed, came to the tomb. It was a cave, and a stone was lying against it. Jesus said, "Take away the stone." Martha, the sister of the dead man, said to him, "Lord, already there is a stench because he has been dead for four days." Jesus said to her, "Did I not tell you that if you believed, you would see the glory of God?" So they took away the stone. And Jesus looked upwards and said, "Father, I thank you for having heard me. I knew that you always hear me, but I have said this for the sake of the crowd standing here, so that they may believe that you sent me." When he had said this, he cried with a loud voice, "Lazarus, come out!" The dead man came out, his hands and feet bound with strips of cloth, and his face wrapped in a cloth. Jesus said to them, "Unbind him, and let him go."

Many of the Jews therefore, who had come with Mary and had seen what Jesus did, believed in him.

Notice what you think and feel as you read the gospel.

Fearlessly, Jesus moves among the people and here does one of his greatest miracles, raising Lazarus from the grave. Seeing it, many of the mourners at the tomb believe in Jesus. In his grief, Jesus shows his love for his friend. In his prayer, he shows his union with his Father.

Pray as you are led for yourself and others.

"Lord, you will also raise me from death to everlasting life. I feel you asking me to pray for those who do not yet believe in you. I think of these . . ." (Continue in your own words.)

Listen to Jesus.

Your life is a walk of faith, my child. But do not cling to your faith; cling to me, for I am your Resurrection and your Life. I also hold in my hand those for whom you pray. What else is Jesus saying to you?

Ask God to show you how to live today.

"I offer myself to you today, Lord, to use me as you will. I want to serve and please you, but I cannot unless you work through me. Work through me, Jesus. Amen."

Monday, April 3, 2017

**Know that God is present
with you and ready to converse.**

"Lord, write on my heart your laws of love. I thank you for your presence here now."

Read the gospel: John 8:1–11.

Jesus went to the Mount of Olives. Early in the morning he came again to the temple. All the people came to him and he sat down and began to teach them. The scribes and the Pharisees brought a woman who had been caught in adultery; and making her stand before all of them, they said to him, "Teacher, this woman was caught in the very act of committing adultery. Now in the law Moses commanded us to stone such women. Now what do you say?" They said this to test him, so that they might have some charge to bring against him. Jesus bent down and wrote with his finger on the ground. When they kept on questioning him, he straightened up and said to them, "Let anyone among you who is without sin be the first to throw a stone at her." And once again he bent down and wrote on the ground. When they heard it, they went away, one by one, beginning with the elders; and Jesus was left alone with the woman standing before him. Jesus straightened up and said to her, "Woman, where are they? Has no one condemned you?" She said, "No one, sir." And Jesus said, "Neither do I condemn you. Go your way, and from now on do not sin again."

Notice what you think and feel as you read the gospel.

The story of the woman taken in adultery seems to illuminate several principles. First, the law of Moses needs to be open to interpretation in its application to specific cases. Second, we should focus our moral scrutiny on ourselves before we judge and condemn others. Third, the Lord is full of mercy and forgiveness of sin. Fourth, the Lord asks the sinner to turn from sin and to obey the law of Moses.

Pray as you are led for yourself and others.

"Lord, my heart is quick to judge others and to excuse myself. By your Spirit, let me seek your forgiveness and let me show only mercy to others. Instead of condemnation, I have mercy upon . . ." (Continue in your own words.)

Listen to Jesus.

Beloved, you strive for much that is contrary to the human heart. You are right to seek holiness by my Spirit, for only in God is it possible to achieve true mercy. What else is Jesus saying to you?

Ask God to show you how to live today.

"Open my eyes and mind to how I can be judgmental. Lord, show me how to put my judgments far from me, case by case. All praise to you, Lord Jesus Christ. Amen."

Tuesday, April 4, 2017

Know that God is present with you and ready to converse.

"Master of the Universe, Holy Trinity, One God, I cannot take you in. Take me into yourself. Capture me by your Word."

Read the gospel: John 8:21–30.

Again Jesus said to them, "I am going away, and you will search for me, but you will die in your sin. Where I am going, you cannot come." Then the Jews said, "Is he going to kill himself? Is that what he means by saying, 'Where I am going, you cannot come'?" He said to them, "You are from below, I am from above; you are of this world, I am not of this world. I told you that you would die in your sins, for you will die in your sins unless you believe that I am he." They said to him, "Who are you?" Jesus said to them, "Why do I speak to you at all? I have much to say about you and much to condemn; but the one who sent me is true, and I declare to the world what I have heard from him." They did not understand that he was speaking to them about the Father. So Jesus said, "When you have lifted up the Son of Man, then you will realize that I am he, and that I do nothing on my own, but I speak these things as the Father instructed me. And the one who sent me is with me; he has not left me alone, for I always do what is pleasing to him." As he was saying these things, many believed in him.

Notice what you think and feel as you read the gospel.

Jesus is thinking of his passion, death, resurrection, and ascension. He shows urgency on behalf of his hearers. He warns them they will die in their sins because they are worldly while he is from heaven, the obedient Son of the Father. He exhorts them to believe in him lest they die in their sins. He tells them they will realize who he is when they lift him up on the Cross.

Pray as you are led for yourself and others.

"Lord, I know I am of this world, full of human weakness. Let me believe and come to you. I pray for all those who resist you . . ." (Continue in your own words.)

Listen to Jesus.

Your faithfulness to me touches me, dear friend. You want others to know your peace in knowing me. Our prayers for them have power with our Father. Thank you for praying with me. What else is Jesus saying to you?

Ask God to show you how to live today.

"I offer you all my thoughts, words, deeds, joys, and sorrows this day that you may count them as a prayer for those you have given me. Keep my mind on you. Amen."

Wednesday, April 5, 2017

**Know that God is present
with you and ready to converse.**

"Jesus, give me your Spirit to know your truth and freedom."

Read the gospel: John 8:31–38 (Jn 8:31–42).

Then Jesus said to the Jews who had believed in him, "If you continue in my word, you are truly my disciples; and you will know the truth, and the truth will make you free." They answered him, "We are descendants of Abraham and have never been slaves to anyone. What do you mean by saying, 'You will be made free'?"

Jesus answered them, "Very truly, I tell you, everyone who commits sin is a slave to sin. The slave does not have a permanent place in the household; the son has a place there forever. So if the Son makes you free, you will be free indeed. I know that you are descendants of Abraham; yet you look for an opportunity to kill me, because there is no place in you for my word. I declare what I have seen in the Father's presence; as for you, you should do what you have heard from the Father."

Notice what you think and feel as you read the gospel.

Jesus declares the truth of his Word: it will make us free. How will we be free? Free from sin. Loving God the Father is also loving Jesus.

Pray as you are led for yourself and others.

"Jesus, let me use the freedom you give me to avoid sin. Let me love God and desire to please God in all things. I wish to help others to see the truth of your

Word and person, Jesus . . ." (Continue in your own words.)

Listen to Jesus.

Examine your life, beloved disciple, in the light of my Word and the freedom it gives you. As you give yourself to me, turning from sin, you will rejoice in the love of God. What else is Jesus saying to you?

Ask God to show you how to live today.

"How am I free, Lord? Make me aware of moments of freedom in this day so that I may choose goodness, truth, love, and God. Amen."

Thursday, April 6, 2017

Know that God is present
with you and ready to converse.

"You are here with me now, Jesus. You are always with me. Let me know you in your Word and carry you forth into my day by your Spirit."

Read the gospel: John 8:51–59.

Jesus said, "Very truly, I tell you, whoever keeps my word will never see death." The Jews said to him, "Now we know that you have a demon. Abraham died, and so did the prophets; yet you say, 'Whoever keeps my word will never taste death.' Are you greater than our father Abraham, who died? The prophets also died. Who do you claim to be?" Jesus answered, "If

I glorify myself, my glory is nothing. It is my Father who glorifies me, he of whom you say, 'He is our God,' though you do not know him. But I know him; if I were to say that I do not know him, I would be a liar like you. But I do know him and I keep his word. Your ancestor Abraham rejoiced that he would see my day; he saw it and was glad." Then the Jews said to him, "You are not yet fifty years old, and have you seen Abraham?" Jesus said to them, "Very truly, I tell you, before Abraham was, I am." So they picked up stones to throw at him, but Jesus hid himself and went out of the temple.

Notice what you think and feel as you read the gospel.

The Jews scorn Jesus' claims of having a special relationship with God, his Father, and his claims of conferring eternal life to those who keep his Word. Jesus puts himself above Abraham, for before Abraham was, Jesus existed. He knows they will turn on him for what seems blasphemy to them, but he is compelled to tell the truth about himself.

Pray as you are led for yourself and others.

"Word of the Father, Light of the World, grant me your Life, your Truth, your Way. I glorify you for your goodness and your generous grace to me and mine . . ." (Continue in your own words.)

Listen to Jesus.

My Father glorified my suffering. I obeyed God for love because God's purposes are all love. Let love operate in your life, child, and God will glorify your suffering as well. What else is Jesus saying to you?

Ask God to show you how to live today.

"I do suffer, Lord, in small and great ways as the days pass. I offer this suffering to our Father for love of those you have given me. Let me love as you do, Jesus. Amen."

Friday, April 7, 2017

Know that God is present with you and ready to converse.

"Jesus, Son of the Father and one with the Father in the unity of the Holy Spirit, lift me to God by your Word."

Read the gospel: John 10:31–39 (Jn 10:31–42).

The Jews took up stones again to stone him. Jesus replied, "I have shown you many good works from the Father. For which of these are you going to stone me?" The Jews answered, "It is not for a good work that we are going to stone you, but for blasphemy, because you, though only a human being, are making yourself God." Jesus answered, "Is it not written in your law, 'I said, you are gods'? If those to whom the word of God came were called 'gods'—and the scripture cannot be annulled—can you say that the one whom the Father has sanctified and sent into the world is blaspheming because I said, 'I am God's Son'? If I am not doing the works of my Father, then do not believe me. But if I do them, even though you do not believe me, believe the works, so that you may know and understand that the Father is in me and I am in the Father." Then they tried to arrest him again, but he escaped from their hands.

Notice what you think and feel as you read the gospel.

Jesus faces stoning by the many who cannot abide the notion that he is God's Son. Jesus appeals to scripture and then to his mighty works as reasons to believe in him. He affirms again that the Father is in him and he is in the Father. He escapes arrest.

Pray as you are led for yourself and others.

"Lord, what is the difference between those who believe your Word and those who don't? I believe. Help my unbelief. I pray for those who do not believe or who suffer from doubts . . ." (Continue in your own words.)

Listen to Jesus.

Your faith is my gift to you, beloved disciple. Treasure it. Put it to use in your prayers and in your actions. Let it grow and bear fruit. What else is Jesus saying to you?

Ask God to show you how to live today.

"Lord, today when I find myself in a situation in which I may act on faith in God, let me do so. Let me remember your words to me and walk in the faith you have given me. Amen."

Saturday, April 8, 2017

Know that God is present with you and ready to converse.

"I am looking for you, Jesus, and ask you to let me find you, know you, and love you in your Word. Speak to me, Lord."

Read the gospel: John 11:45–53 (Jn 11:45–56).

Many of the Jews therefore, who had come with Mary and had seen what Jesus did, believed in him. But some of them went to the Pharisees and told them what he had done. So the chief priests and the Pharisees called a meeting of the council, and said, "What are we to do? This man is performing many signs. If we let him go on like this, everyone will believe in him, and the Romans will come and destroy both our holy place and our nation." But one of them, Caiaphas, who was high priest that year, said to them, "You know nothing at all! You do not understand that it is better for you to have one man die for the people than to have the whole nation destroyed." He did not say this on his own, but being high priest that year he prophesied that Jesus was about to die for the nation, and not for the nation only, but to gather into one the dispersed children of God. So from that day on they planned to put him to death.

Notice what you think and feel as you read the gospel.

Feeling threatened by the many who believe in Jesus, the Pharisees call a meeting. They are worried that the many conversions to Jesus will provoke the Romans to destroy their religious traditions. The chief priest, Caiaphas, suggests that Jesus may make a good scapegoat for the nation; his comment is truer than he realized at the time.

Pray as you are led for yourself and others.

"Jesus, you hide yourself and you show yourself in obedience to God, not for fear of others. Let me be as you were, led only by the will of God. Give me grace to do God's will . . ." (continue in your own words.)

Listen to Jesus.

Servant of God, I come to you with love this moment, and I will be close to you all day. As you give yourself to God, God's will is done. Follow me. What else is Jesus saying to you?

Ask God to show you how to live today.

"Jesus, you came to earth and changed history. Work with me in my life to change things, that I may hasten the coming of the kingdom of God. Thank you. Amen."

HOLY WEEK

Let us run to accompany him as he hastens toward his passion, and imitate those who met him then, not by covering his path with garments, olive branches, or palms, but by doing all we can to prostrate ourselves before him by being humble and trying to live as he would wish. Then we shall be able to receive the Word at his coming, and God, whom no limits can contain, will be within us.

St. Andrew of Crete
Office of Readings
Passion Sunday

Sunday, April 9, 2017
Palm Sunday of the Lord's Passion

Know that God is present
with you and ready to converse.

The story of God made flesh, coming into the world to proclaim his Father's love for all humanity and to save us from sin and death now turns grim. Jesus faces his destiny: to be captured, tortured, and crucified by his enemies while also abandoned by his friends. What do these awful events mean? The Word is open to us that we may understand.

"Jesus, let me enter into your passion with open eyes and heart that I may love you more and serve you better than I ever have."

Read the gospel: Matthew
27:24–37, 45–54 (Mt 26:14–27:66).

So when Pilate saw that he could do nothing, but rather that a riot was beginning, he took some water and washed his hands before the crowd, saying, "I am innocent of this man's blood; see to it yourselves." Then the people as a whole answered, "His blood be on us and on our children." So he released Barabbas for them; and after flogging Jesus, he handed him over to be crucified.

Then the soldiers of the governor took Jesus into the governor's headquarters, and they gathered the whole cohort around him. They stripped him and put a scarlet robe on him, and after twisting some thorns

into a crown, they put it on his head. They put a reed
in his right hand and knelt before him and mocked
him, saying, "Hail, King of the Jews!" They spat on
him, and took the reed and struck him on the head.
After mocking him, they stripped him of the robe and
put his own clothes on him. Then they led him away
to crucify him.

As they went out, they came upon a man from
Cyrene named Simon; they compelled this man to
carry his cross. And when they came to a place called
Golgotha (which means Place of a Skull), they offered
him wine to drink, mixed with gall; but when he tasted
it, he would not drink it. And when they had crucified him, they divided his clothes among themselves
by casting lots; then they sat down there and kept
watch over him. Over his head they put the charge
against him, which read, "This is Jesus, the King of
the Jews." . . .

From noon on, darkness came over the whole land
until three in the afternoon. And about three o'clock
Jesus cried with a loud voice, "Eli, Eli, lema sabach-
thani?" that is, "My God, my God, why have you for-
saken me?" When some of the bystanders heard it,
they said, "This man is calling for Elijah." At once one
of them ran and got a sponge, filled it with sour wine,
put it on a stick, and gave it to him to drink. But the
others said, "Wait, let us see whether Elijah will come
to save him." Then Jesus cried again with a loud voice
and breathed his last. At that moment the curtain of
the temple was torn in two, from top to bottom. The
earth shook, and the rocks were split. The tombs also

were opened, and many bodies of the saints who had fallen asleep were raised. After his resurrection they came out of the tombs and entered the holy city and appeared to many. Now when the centurion and those with him, who were keeping watch over Jesus, saw the earthquake and what took place, they were terrified and said, "Truly this man was God's Son!"

Notice what you think and feel as you read the gospel.

This is an account of Jesus' passion. He is arrested, flogged, crowned with thorns, stripped, forced to carry his Cross, and crucified. This is what Jesus had come to do.

Pray as you are led for yourself and others.

"Lord, I have desired to follow you. Help me to take up my own cross and follow you all the way to God. What a privilege you give me that I can join you in acts of love . . ." (Continue in your own words.)

Listen to Jesus.

You will be tried and tested, dearest beloved, as I was. Turn to me, for I have power to redeem your sufferings. By them, you will glorify God and help others. Continue in my love. What else is Jesus saying to you?

Ask God to show you how to live today.

"God, I cannot face suffering unless you are with me. Be with me. Be with all who suffer. Let us not suffer needlessly but for the good of ourselves and others. Amen."

Monday, April 10, 2017

**Know that God is present
with you and ready to converse.**

"Jesus, Word of the Father, enter my heart, mind, soul, and spirit as I read and pray today."

Read the gospel: Luke 4:16–21.

When Jesus came to Nazareth, where he had been brought up, he went to the synagogue on the sabbath day, as was his custom. He stood up to read, and the scroll of the prophet Isaiah was given to him. He unrolled the scroll and found the place where it was written:

"The Spirit of the Lord is upon me,
because he has anointed me
to bring good news to the poor.
He has sent me to proclaim release to the captives
and recovery of sight to the blind,
to let the oppressed go free,
to proclaim the year of the Lord's favor."

And he rolled up the scroll, gave it back to the attendant, and sat down. The eyes of all in the synagogue were fixed on him. Then he began to say to them, "Today this scripture has been fulfilled in your hearing."

Notice what you think and feel as you read the gospel.

What a stunning event for those who attended the synagogue of Nazareth that day! Here the young man Jesus, whom they all knew well, stands up to read the prophetic words of Isaiah. The Messiah would bring good news to the poor, release captives, give sight to the blind, and free the oppressed. Who is this Messiah? Jesus says it is he.

Pray as you are led for yourself and others.

"Lord, fill me with wonder that you are real, true God made man, the Savior of the world. Be my Savior, too, Lord, today and tomorrow. Extend your mercy upon . . ." (Continue in your own words.)

Listen to Jesus.

If you want to know who you are, beloved, follow me. No one else is like you. That is why I love you and need you to be who you are. What else is Jesus saying to you?

Ask God to show you how to live today.

"Lord, you declared your identity clearly at the start of your ministry. Help me be genuine, authentic, and honest with myself and all I encounter, for that is what you call me to do. Thank you. Amen."

Tuesday, April 11, 2017

Know that God is present
with you and ready to converse.

"Jesus, let me know you better so that I may follow you
more closely. Teach me by your Word."

Read the gospel: John 13:21–33, 36–38.

After saying this Jesus was troubled in spirit, and
declared, "Very truly, I tell you, one of you will betray
me." The disciples looked at one another, uncertain
of whom he was speaking. One of his disciples—the
one whom Jesus loved—was reclining next to him;
Simon Peter therefore motioned to him to ask Jesus
of whom he was speaking. So while reclining next to
Jesus, he asked him, "Lord, who is it?" Jesus answered,
"It is the one to whom I give this piece of bread when
I have dipped it in the dish." So when he had dipped
the piece of bread, he gave it to Judas son of Simon
Iscariot. After he received the piece of bread, Satan
entered into him. Jesus said to him, "Do quickly what
you are going to do." Now no one at the table knew
why he said this to him. Some thought that, because
Judas had the common purse, Jesus was telling him,
"Buy what we need for the festival"; or, that he should
give something to the poor. So, after receiving the piece
of bread, he immediately went out. And it was night.

When he had gone out, Jesus said, "Now the Son
of Man has been glorified, and God has been glorified
in him. If God has been glorified in him, God will also

glorify him in himself and will glorify him at once. Little children, I am with you only a little longer. You will look for me; and as I said to the Jews so now I say to you, 'Where I am going, you cannot come.'" . . .

Simon Peter said to him, "Lord, where are you going?" Jesus answered, "Where I am going, you cannot follow me now; but you will follow afterwards." Peter said to him, "Lord, why can I not follow you now? I will lay down my life for you." Jesus answered, "Will you lay down your life for me? Very truly, I tell you, before the cock crows, you will have denied me three times."

Notice what you think and feel as you read the gospel.

Jesus begins the evening of the Passover troubled by his impending betrayal, but when Judas finally goes out, Jesus speaks of his glory and his coming departure to a place they cannot follow. Peter protests, but Jesus predicts his denial. Yet Peter would follow Jesus, laying down his life.

Pray as you are led for yourself and others.

"Lord, I have denied you, and I'm sorry. But I ask you to let me follow you, dying to myself and forsaking all for you. Show me how to do that . . ." (Continue in your own words.)

Listen to Jesus.

If I am the love of your life, if you give your whole heart to me, I will guide you in my path of service. Will you suffer? Yes, but you will also share my glory. What else is Jesus saying to you?

Ask God to show you how to live today.

"Help me to get my eyes off of myself, Lord, and look upon you, the crucified and risen King of Glory. I praise your holy name. Amen."

Wednesday, April 12, 2017

Know that God is present with you and ready to converse.

"Lord, I have been close to you, and you are with me now. Keep me from all betrayal; let me never turn away from you."

Read the gospel: Matthew 26:14–25.

Then one of the twelve, who was called Judas Iscariot, went to the chief priests and said, "What will you give me if I betray him to you?" They paid him thirty pieces of silver. And from that moment he began to look for an opportunity to betray him.

On the first day of Unleavened Bread the disciples came to Jesus, saying, "Where do you want us to make the preparations for you to eat the Passover?" He said, "Go into the city to a certain man, and say to him, 'The

Teacher says, My time is near; I will keep the Passover at your house with my disciples.'" So the disciples did as Jesus had directed them, and they prepared the Passover meal.

When it was evening, he took his place with the twelve; and while they were eating, he said, "Truly I tell you, one of you will betray me." And they became greatly distressed and began to say to him one after another, "Surely not I, Lord?" He answered, "The one who has dipped his hand into the bowl with me will betray me. The Son of Man goes as it is written of him, but woe to that one by whom the Son of Man is betrayed! It would have been better for that one not to have been born." Judas, who betrayed him, said, "Surely not I, Rabbi?" He replied, "You have said so."

Notice what you think and feel as you read the gospel.

Judas, though he had traveled with Jesus, heard his preaching, seen his miracles, and was given a position of trust, agrees to betray Jesus to the chief priests for money. All people are subject to temptation. He must have deluded himself about what he was doing. He lied to the Lord.

Pray as you are led for yourself and others.

"Lord, let me never forget that I am weak, easily tempted to value things other than you. In my weakness, love me and let me do what pleases you . . ." (Continue in your own words.)

Listen to Jesus.

I do love you, my dear child. Open yourself in all your failure and weakness to me. I understand. I will wash and heal you and make you strong. What else is Jesus saying to you?

Ask God to show you how to live today.

"I need you, Lord. Today I need you to see well, to love well, to speak well, and to do well. Thank you. Amen."

Thursday, April 13, 2017
Holy Thursday

Know that God is present with you and ready to converse.

"Jesus, Son of the Father, you show me how you live by your Word. Let your lessons be bound to my heart."

Read the gospel: John 13:2b–15 (Jn 13:1–15).

And during supper Jesus, knowing that the Father had given all things into his hands, and that he had come from God and was going to God, got up from the table, took off his outer robe, and tied a towel around himself. Then he poured water into a basin and began to wash the disciples' feet and to wipe them with the towel that was tied around him. He came to Simon Peter, who said to him, "Lord, are you going to wash my feet?" Jesus answered, "You do not know now what I am doing, but later you will understand." Peter said to him, "You will never wash my feet." Jesus answered, "Unless I wash you, you have no share with me." Simon Peter said to him, "Lord, not my feet only but also my hands and my head!" Jesus said to him, "One who has bathed does not need to wash, except for the feet, but is entirely clean. And you are clean, though not all of you." For he knew who was to betray him; for this reason he said, "Not all of you are clean."

After he had washed their feet, had put on his robe, and had returned to the table, he said to them, "Do you know what I have done to you? You call me Teacher and Lord—and you are right, for that is what I am. So if I, your Lord and Teacher, have washed your feet, you also ought to wash one another's feet. For I have set you an example, that you also should do as I have done to you."

Notice what you think and feel as you read the gospel.

Jesus teaches by example that the greatest ones will wash the feet of those they serve. Not just in the washing of the feet but throughout his ministry Jesus served others.

Pray as you are led for yourself and others.

"How shall I put your lesson into action, Lord? These are people I intend to serve, so help me God . . ." (Continue in your own words.)

Listen to Jesus.

You will find great joy in humble service. Don't talk about it. Don't pat yourself on the back. You are only doing what I have commanded. What else is Jesus saying to you?

Ask God to show you how to live today.

"Give me the skill, Jesus, to know how to serve others without embarrassing them or striking a false pose of humility. Amen."

Friday, April 14, 2017
Friday of the Passion
of the Lord (Good Friday)

**Know that God is present
with you and ready to converse.**

"Lord, I come to you on this day with awe and trembling. You willingly went to your death for love of me."

**Read the gospel: John 19:25b–37
(Jn 18:1–19:42).**

Meanwhile, standing near the cross of Jesus were his mother, and his mother's sister, Mary the wife of Clopas, and Mary Magdalene. When Jesus saw his mother and the disciple whom he loved standing beside her, he said to his mother, "Woman, here is your son." Then he said to the disciple, "Here is your mother." And from that hour the disciple took her into his own home.

After this, when Jesus knew that all was now finished, he said (in order to fulfill the scripture), "I am thirsty." A jar full of sour wine was standing there. So they put a sponge full of the wine on a branch of hyssop and held it to his mouth. When Jesus had received the wine, he said, "It is finished." Then he bowed his head and gave up his spirit.

Since it was the day of Preparation, the Jews did not want the bodies left on the cross during the sabbath, especially because that sabbath was a day of great solemnity. So they asked Pilate to have the legs of the crucified men broken and the bodies removed. Then the soldiers came and broke the legs of the first and of the other who had been crucified with him. But when they came to Jesus and saw that he was already dead, they did not break his legs. Instead, one of the soldiers pierced his side with a spear, and at once blood and water came out. (He who saw this has testified so that you also may believe. His testimony is true, and he knows that he tells the truth.) These things occurred so that the scripture might be fulfilled, "None of his bones shall be broken." And again another passage of scripture says, "They will look on the one whom they have pierced."

Notice what you think and feel as you read the gospel.

How brave and good Jesus was throughout that horrible ordeal, his torture and death. In the end, blood and water flowed out of his pierced side.

Pray as you are led for yourself and others.

"Jesus, I am not worthy, but you died for love of me. Let me be washed clean of all sin by your blood. Let me thank you and glorify you this moment . . ." (Continue in your own words.)

Listen to Jesus.

My child, I love you now as I loved you then. Do you love me? What else is Jesus saying to you?

Ask God to show you how to live today.

"Lord, I am burdened and broken by my own crosses, even today. Give me your courage and your heart to journey today until the end. Amen."

Saturday, April 15, 2017
Holy Saturday

Know that God is present
with you and ready to converse.

"Jesus, you live. Live in me and guide me by your Word."

Read the gospel: Matthew 28:1–10.

After the sabbath, as the first day of the week was dawning, Mary Magdalene and the other Mary went to see the tomb. And suddenly there was a great earthquake; for an angel of the Lord, descending from heaven, came and rolled back the stone and sat on it. His appearance was like lightning, and his clothing white as snow. For fear of him the guards shook and became like dead men. But the angel said to the women, "Do not be afraid; I know that you are looking for Jesus who was crucified. He is not here; for he has been raised, as he said. Come, see the place where he lay. Then go quickly and tell his disciples, 'He has been raised from the dead, and indeed he is going ahead of you to Galilee; there you will see him.' This is my message for you." So they left the tomb quickly with fear and great joy, and ran to tell his disciples. Suddenly Jesus met them and said, "Greetings!" And they came to him, took hold of his feet, and worshipped him. Then Jesus said to them, "Do not be afraid; go and tell my brothers to go to Galilee; there they will see me."

Notice what you think and feel as you read the gospel.

The women are the first to know and believe Jesus is alive. They understood. They worshipped. They obeyed.

Pray as you are led for yourself and others.

"Lord, strengthen my faith in the miracle of your resurrection. Let it be so real to me that the living Jesus becomes the center of my life. Let others see you through me . . ." (Continue in your own words.)

Listen to Jesus.

I take care of you, beloved. Trust in me. Let others know you do. Ask me for whatever you need. What else is Jesus saying to you?

Ask God to show you how to live today.

"Show me in many little ways how to recognize you, worship you, and obey you. I need you, Lord. Amen."

Sunday, April 16, 2017
Easter Sunday

Know that God is present
with you and ready to converse.

After his passion, death, and burial, Jesus rises bodily from the dead. This is the fulfillment of his ministry on earth. What he had told his disciples would happen has happened. They cannot easily take it in. But they come to believe this great mystery.

"Risen Lord, you have revealed yourself to many. Reveal yourself to me."

Read the gospel: John 20:1–9.

Early on the first day of the week, while it was still dark, Mary Magdalene came to the tomb and saw that the stone had been removed from the tomb. So she ran and went to Simon Peter and the other disciple, the one whom Jesus loved, and said to them, "They have taken the Lord out of the tomb, and we do not know

where they have laid him." Then Peter and the other
disciple set out and went towards the tomb. The two
were running together, but the other disciple outran
Peter and reached the tomb first. He bent down to look
in and saw the linen wrappings lying there, but he did
not go in. Then Simon Peter came, following him, and
went into the tomb. He saw the linen wrappings lying
there, and the cloth that had been on Jesus' head, not
lying with the linen wrappings but rolled up in a place
by itself. Then the other disciple, who reached the tomb
first, also went in, and he saw and believed; for as yet
they did not understand the scripture, that he must
rise from the dead.

Notice what you think
and feel as you read the gospel.

The scene in the tomb with the wrappings and the
head cloth is very specific. When the other disciple,
John, sees it, he believes.

Pray as you are led for yourself and others.

"The world has never seen such a miracle as your resurrection, Lord. Alleluia! You are my Shepherd and
you will lead me into your life . . ." (Continue in your
own words.)

Listen to Jesus.

*You may follow me with confidence, dear one. With me you
will do well, and those around you will notice.* What else
is Jesus saying to you?

Ask God to show you how to live today.

"I would like to help others believe in you, Lord. Let me see the opportunities to say and do things that reveal you. You are one with Almighty God, Father, Son, and Holy Spirit. Amen."

Please Take Our Survey!
Now that you've finished reading *Sacred Reading for Lent 2017*, please go to **avemariapress.com/feedback** to take a brief survey about your experience. Ave Maria Press and the Apostleship of Prayer appreciate your feedback.

The Apostleship of Prayer is an international Jesuit prayer ministry that reaches more than 35 million members worldwide through its popular website, apostleshipofprayer.org, and through talks, conferences, publications, and retreats. Known as "the pope's worldwide prayer network," the Apostleship's mission is to encourage Christians to make a daily offering of themselves to the Lord in union with the Sacred Heart of Jesus.

Douglas Leonard is executive director of the Apostleship of Prayer in the United States, where he has served since 2006. He earned a bachelor's degree in English in 1976, a master's degree in English in 1977, and a doctorate in English in 1981, all from the University of Wisconsin-Madison. Leonard also has served in higher education, professional development, publishing, and instructional design as an executive, writer, editor, educator, and consultant.